Praise for *If You Could See as Jesus Sees*

"At times we all struggle with our identity and mistakenly base our worth on performance and trying to measure up to an ever-changing standard. Elizabeth Oates shows us how the lenses we choose to look through color our view and determine our so-called 'truth.' May this book help you see yourself rightly by looking through the lenses of Christ. And, by knowing His great love and acceptance, set you free from self!"
—Kristen Hatton, blogger and author, *Get Your Story Straight: A Teen Guide for Learning and Living the Gospel*

"This is an excellent book for women to read in community and open their eyes to the reality that they are dearly beloved daughters of God."
—Dr. Deborah Newman, Minister to Women, Park Cities Baptist Church, author, counselor

"Do you. . .compare yourself with the social-media versions of your friends and acquaintances? Berate yourself when your neighbor wins parent of the year? Let yourself get sucked into the vacuum of performance and comparison? If you struggle with identity and worth issues, Elizabeth Oates is a kind companion who has walked that same road. And she has a message: You can find hope for yourself and those you influence by seeing yourself as Jesus sees you."
—Dr. Sandra Glahn, seminary professor and author of The Coffee Cup Bible Study series

"In the words of Dr. Martin Luther King Jr., 'Hatred darkens life; love illuminates it.' With vulnerability and personal transparency, Elizabeth Oates gently guides women beyond the self-loathing darkness of negative self-talk into the illuminating light of Christ filled with love, beauty, acceptance, and belonging from darkness to light, from how the wo nispers Jesus' words to women battling all that 'My grace is sufficient for you weakness.'"

— R. Scott Gornto, author of *The Stories We Tell Ourselves*

"Elizabeth's offering is more of a war cry of women searching for significance. She bravely outs the enemy's tactics and refutes them with the hardest hitting weapon we have, the Word of God, just like Jesus did in the desert. I was moved to tears while reading the pages, resonating with the understanding that if women really 'get this,' there will be an army of whole, satisfied, gloriously liberated troops ready to make the ordinary days miraculous and unafraid to shape culture toward Kingdom!"

—Emily Mills, founder and co-CEO of Jesus Said Love

"Knowing that you are not alone in your struggle is an issue that all women face, and Elizabeth helps us feel [better] about our inadequacies and our struggles. . . . Get ready for a journey that will change the way you see yourself and others around you."

—Deanna Nail, founder and chief inspirer, Serendipity Ministries

Elizabeth Oates

If You
Could See
as
Jesus
Sees

Inspiration for a Life of
Hope, Joy, and Purpose

SHILOH RUN PRESS
An Imprint of Barbour Publishing, Inc.

Print ISBN 978-1-63409-512-9

eBook Editions:
Adobe Digital Edition (.epub) 978-1-63409-733-8
Kindle and MobiPocket Edition (.prc) 978-1-63409-734-5

Published in association with the literary agency of Credo Communications, LLC, Grand Rapids, Michigan, www.credocommunications.net.

Published by Shiloh Run Press, an imprint of Barbour Publishing, Inc., P.O. Box 719, Uhrichsville, Ohio 44683, www.shilohrunpress.com

Our mission is to publish and distribute inspirational products offering exceptional value and biblical encouragement to the masses.

Member of the
Evangelical Christian
Publishers Association

Printed in the United States of America.

Contents

Dedication

To Clarey and CeCe
May you always see as Jesus sees

Acknowledgments

- Brandon – How can I thank you for your constant support and encouragement, for never letting me quit, and for always taking care of our plethora of children while I wrote this book? Most of all, thank you for reminding me that, "We are on the same team."

- Carter, Clarey, and Campbell – Thank you for eating countless dinners of chicken nuggets, hot dogs, and pizza while your mom ignored you, night after night, while hiding in my closet and pecking away at my computer. You are selfless and understanding and I want to be like you when I grow up. Thank you for teaching me what I should be teaching you.

- CeCe – You joined our family one month before I received this book contract and all I could think was, "Seriously, God? You're giving me a baby and a book contract at the *same time*?" Little did I know God was giving us the sweetest, most flexible, most gracious baby on earth. You let me sleep through the night and God gave me lots of energy to write and love you during the day. Thank you for teaching us how to live in the moment and to treasure each day. You are such a gift! Isaiah 43:19

- To my extended family – Thank you for your support during my writing journey. Everyone needs a cheering section, and I am so glad you are mine.

- My BAM sistahs – One of you recently posted a quote that said, "The most memorable people in life will be the friends who loved you when you weren't very loveable." This certainly describes the way you have loved and pursued me: fervently, consistently, and unconditionally. I am grateful for each one of you and you will always be my sistahs. And my BAMs.

- Stephanie, Rose, Beth, Kyna, and Martha Kate – Thank you for sharing your stories with such honesty and vulnerability. My prayer is that women everywhere will find hope and healing because of your bravery.

- Katy, Sarah B, Kelly, Jordan, Rachel, Liz, Brett, Emily, and Joey – I always tell people, "If you are my friend, beware. You just might end up in an article, blog, or book someday." I guess this was your day. Thank you for allowing me to include you in this project. You have obviously made an impact on me, and I know you will make an impact on others as well!

- Taylor Jackson – Thank you for your insightful editing skills. You are talented and gifted and have a bright future ahead of you. I can't wait to see where the Lord uses you. Please remember me when you bypass me in the world of writing!

- Karen Neumair and Tim Credo – Thank you for believing in me enough to sign me as a client. I am so grateful for your confidence in me as a writer. Karen, you are wise, perceptive, diplomatic, and calm. . .basically everything I am not! You are an outstanding agent, and I am so thankful to you for steering me in the right direction at every single turn.

- To Kelly McIntosh and the entire team at Shiloh Run Press – Thank you for all your diligence, time, and effort on this project. Thank you for entrusting it to me and making me a part of the Barbour team!

Note to Group Leaders

Thank you for taking on the privilege and responsibility of leading a group of women through *If You Could See as Jesus Sees*. The next ten chapters may uncover areas of both pain and strength for the women in your flock. You will have the honor of walking alongside them as they unpack years of memories, injury, and discomfort that will hopefully lead them into a closer, stronger, and more dynamic relationship with Jesus. My prayer for every woman who picks up this book is that she would see herself not as the world sees her and not as she sees herself, but as Jesus sees her.

Two things to note:

- Pace your group. Some groups will share freely while others take awhile to openly discuss their feelings and ideas. Be patient with your group and do not be discouraged if your group takes longer to open up than other groups.
- Each chapter contains two sets of questions: Personal Reflection Questions and Group Reflection Questions. Feel free to walk your group through both sets of questions; however, please note that the Personal Reflection Questions are more private in nature. Depending on the level of intimacy in your group, not everyone may feel comfortable sharing. Gauge your own group and ask questions accordingly.

Joy in the journey,
Elizabeth

Introduction

The majority of the time I spent writing *If You Could See as Jesus Sees*, the enemy whispered seeds of doubt in my ear. "Who are you to write this book? You're not good enough. You're not wise enough. You're not popular enough. You're not funny enough."

The sad thing is, I believed him.

I believed every word, every lie, every bit of darkness he used to eclipse my light. While writing a book on God's truth, I succumbed to the enemy's lies. While writing a book on claiming our identity, I lost my own. While writing a book on freedom, I became enslaved. While writing a book on seeing ourselves through Jesus' eyes, I saw myself through the enemy's eyes, through the world's eyes, and through my own very tearful, defeated eyes. #ironic

As I started talking to other women who felt just like me, I realized I was not alone in my struggle. . . . Duh! Isn't that the point of this book? That we band together in our sisterhood and realize we are not alone in our pain? Together, as we lean into Jesus and embrace His truth, we can begin to see as Jesus sees.

One evening my five-year-old son, Campbell, scraped his big toe in the backyard, the type of injury where the skin was hanging off. (Are you cringing yet?) That night I gave him a bath and told him he needed to soak his toe in the tub.

"No, Mommy!" he screamed. "It's going to hurt!"

"I know, buddy," I told him. "But it will clean your toe and help it get better." Then he got quiet and paused for a moment.

"Oh, I get it," he said thoughtfully. "Sometimes it has to hurt before it heals." Exactly. That is how your journey might play out as you read through this book. Certain parts will be uncomfortable, even painful at times, but sometimes we have to hurt before we heal.

So, let the journey begin. Shall we?

Chapter 1

My Lens of Self-Loathing, His Lens of Love

I remember it vividly. I was in the fourth grade, sitting in a store dressing room with my mom, tears flowing uncontrollably.

"What is wrong?" she asked in bewilderment. One minute we were happily shopping; the next minute I sat in a heap, unable to move or talk. Unfortunately, there were too many problems to articulate. I didn't even know where to begin.

Should I start with the fact that I felt fat? Or that I didn't fit in at school? I was, after all, at my third elementary school in two years. Maybe it was the beginning of raging hormones or the stress of living in a single-parent home. Or maybe it was the perfect storm of all of the above. My life simply felt out of control, and I didn't know how to articulate it at the young age of ten. All I knew was, at that very moment, I hated myself.

For the most part, I pulled out of it. Or so I thought. I masked my insecurities by becoming an overachiever who racked up more good grades and extracurricular activities than Taylor Swift has Grammys.

From the outside, my life looked pristine. Yet on the inside, I constantly wrestled with feelings of self-loathing and self-doubt. Am I pretty enough? Smart enough? Thin enough? Good enough? Successful enough? Am I ever enough? And if I am enough, then enough for whom? Myself? My family? My teachers? My friends? My world? My God?

I have a hunch that I am not alone in this struggle. I think most women—from ages ten to one hundred—wrestle with feelings of inadequacy, doubt, worthlessness, hopelessness, and maybe even self-loathing at some point in their lives. We scorn our bodies, our faces, or our hair. Maybe we even dislike ourselves at our core: our personalities, our gifts, our talents, and our souls. So we spend days, if not years, comparing ourselves to our friends or media celebrities and daydreaming about a different life.

Eventually we morph into an existence vaguely similar to ourselves, yet not quite us. We dress like our friends or emulate what we see in *InStyle* magazine. We change our appearance through plastic surgery. We alter our behavior to please others. Before we know it, we are just an empty shell of our true selves, mere imposters of the women God created.

Why Do We Resent Ourselves?

We must ask, "Why do we resent ourselves?" and "From where does this self-loathing stem?" Why did I sit in that dressing room at age ten crying tears of intense emotional pain? The details vary from girl to girl, from woman to woman. Yet, for each of us, a common thread weaves through our stories: the grand story of the fall.

Think back to Eve in the Garden of Eden. She lived in paradise with her loving husband, Adam, and her devoted God. Adam desired only Eve. Nothing distracted him or stole his attention away from his beautiful bride. Their love was pure and undivided.

They enjoyed constant fellowship with their Creator. They worked for life-giving, soul-sustaining fulfillment and joy—not to pay never-ending bills or rent.

Then the deceitful serpent entered the stage. Listening to his empty promises and twisted propaganda, Eve succumbed to his lies. And we are forever left to pick up the pieces.

The moment Eve succumbed to her desires and took that bite, humanity changed. Scripture tells us that before the fall, "Adam and his wife were both naked, and they felt no shame" (Genesis 2:25). Yet, after the fall, "The Eternal God pieced together the skins of animals and made clothes for Adam and Eve to wear" (Genesis 3:21 THE VOICE).

These two verses tell us that because of Eve's initial decision to surrender to her fleshly wants, we forever bear the burden of shame and guilt—both of which lead to regret and self-loathing.

Genesis also tells us, "So the Eternal God banished Adam and Eve from the garden of Eden and exiled humanity from paradise, sentencing humans to laborious lives working the very ground man came from. After driving them out, He stationed winged guardians at the east end of the garden of Eden and set up a sword of flames, which alertly turned back and forth to guard the way to the tree of life" (Genesis 3:23–24 THE VOICE).

I love these verses in *The Voice* translation because they capture the fact that after the fall, God no longer trusted His children. It says God "stationed winged guardians" to warn Him if Adam and Eve tried to make their way back into the Garden of Eden. Trust broken. Fellowship tainted.

Put yourself in Eve's place for a moment. Can you imagine being responsible for this calamity? Can you imagine making one irrevocable decision that not only separates you from God, but also creates emotional distance between you and your husband and creates tension between your future children? One flawed choice throws the entire human race into a cataclysmic fate, which it spends the rest of eternity trying to remedy.

How do you think Eve felt? Can you get inside her brain, inside her heart, and imagine how badly she ached for her paradise to return? She followed a serpent's leading instead of her husband's counsel. She disobeyed God's direct orders and caused a great rift to come between them. She sinned against humanity and left a wake of destruction for eternity.

We will never know the thoughts racing through Eve's mind or how fast her heart rate increased as she heard God's voice bellow, "What is this you have done?" (Genesis 3:13). But what we do know is that sins like Eve's—and sins like ours—are just one cause that propel women into a downward spiral of self-loathing. And once we enter into this space of self-contempt, it is difficult to pull ourselves out. Difficult, but not impossible. For we know "with God all things are possible" (Matthew 19:26).

The Sins We Commit

Sometimes self-loathing is caused by sins we commit: lies, gossip, betrayal, apathy, adultery, or pride. Like Eve, we bring drama into our lives with decisions and conscious choices we make. Sometimes these choices sneak up on us. Other times our sins are more deliberate—more thought out—and over time, our lives shift into something unrecognizable. Then, like a bad dream, we awake to our senses. We look all around us at the devastating debris we caused, and we weep. Where do we begin cleaning up our mess? Is it even possible? Like Eve's situation, maybe it's not. Maybe there is no shovel large enough to haul away all the rubble. Maybe all we can do is move forward.

We mourn the loss, the pain, and those we hurt. We rectify relationships. We ask for forgiveness. We pursue restoration.

And then we turn inward. We try to heal ourselves. Sometimes we succeed. Yet sometimes the emotional pain and regret overwhelm us. We are unable to forgive ourselves for the pain we caused, for the wounds we inflicted, for the war cry we howled at the top of our lungs. This is when regret turns to self-hatred. We see ourselves through a lens of self-loathing instead of seeing ourselves through Jesus' lens of love and forgiveness.

The Sins People Commit against Us

Sometimes our self-loathing stems from pain inflicted on us by others. This pain takes on many different forms. For example, if we suffered abuse as a child, we might carry that trauma with us into adulthood. If we found ourselves in an abusive relationship with a boyfriend or spouse, those physical and emotional wounds may eventually heal, but the scars remain.

Maybe you were the victim of bullying. Remember the "Burn Book" from the movie *Mean Girls*, starring Tina Fey, Lindsay Lohan, and Rachel McAdams? In this 2004 satirical comedy, the self-absorbed popular girls, "the Plastics," created a sparkly-on-the-outside yet dark-on-the-inside book in which they wrote vicious, hateful, untrue verbiage about their classmates. These lies and rumors eventually leaked to the rest of the school, causing an uprising from the bullied "lower class."

Rumors, lies, and merciless teasing from girls such as the Plastics have now made their way to social media. Today school systems approach bullying with stricter rules and tougher consequences, but when my generation was growing up, administration dismissed things like burn books as rites of passage. Unfortunately, the emotional damage lingers for many women.

Neglect is another issue that results in emotional pain among women today. Generation X is the largest population to grow up in divorced families, with millennials not far behind. Divorced and single-parent homes often lead to neglect—whether intentional or not—as parents rebuild their lives. Mom, who may never have worked outside the home before, is now thrust into the workforce. Dad adjusts to life as a single guy or finds a new family faster than you can say "child support." The children are often left to fend for themselves.

People often say kids are resilient, and they are—especially children from dysfunctional families. Once grown, however, the emotional pain from childhood resurfaces. Significant life events, such as weddings, birthdays, or becoming a new mom, may trigger memories and feelings of neglect that once lay dormant in a woman's heart, mind, and soul.

Wallowing in Darkness

Pain often leads to feelings of anger, bitterness, and hatred. When we live in a place of constant self-loathing, we wallow in darkness. We usually address our resident darkness in one of three ways.

First, we choose to live in Stucksville, where people stay stuck. Paralyzed. Unable to move forward in life. We are unable pursue relationships—romantic or friendly. We cannot heal from past hurts. We cannot grow emotionally or spiritually. We consistently gorge ourselves on a feast of lies the enemy feeds us; then, like a bulimic, we purge them back into the world with our negative thoughts, words, and actions.

We don't believe we are worthy of love or happiness, so we go out of our way to show ourselves contempt. We punish ourselves in many different physical, emotional, and spiritual ways. Do any of these ways look familiar to you?

- We refuse to let ourselves form deep friendships.
- We sabotage relationships.
- We cling to people.
- We become jealous and/or feel threatened when a close friend forms a friendship or romantic relationship with another person.
- We engage in negative self-talk.
- We make self-deprecating jokes about ourselves in front of other people in order to beat them to the punch.
- We develop low self-esteem and eventually view ourselves in an untrue light.
- We can't make decisions.
- We overeat or undereat, which may lead to an eating disorder or on the spectrum of disordered eating.
- We develop body dysmorphic disorder (BDD) (an unhealthy preoccupation with a real or perceived imperfection with our appearance).

Dr. Martin Luther King Jr. once said, "Hatred paralyzes life; love releases it. Hatred confuses life; love harmonizes it. Hatred darkens life; love illumines it." When we hate—even hate ourselves—we live in a state of paralysis, confusion, and darkness. When we love ourselves, we live in freedom, harmony, and light.

If we camp out with self-loathing for too long, eventually it morphs into people-loathing. After all, if we don't like ourselves, how can we like anyone else, including our spouse, our children, our friends, our family, our coworkers, and our neighbors—the very people God has put in our path. The very people to whom God calls us to minister. We will wake up one day to a great divide between us and the rest of the world. Sadly, the chasm was not caused by an earthquake or a freak plane crash, but by our own self-loathing and pride.

The second way we handle living in darkness, or self-loathing, is by choosing to live in a place I like to call Confusedom. Unlike Stucksville, where everyone is incapacitated and unable to move, people in Confusedom mill about from place to place and function within society. People don't spot us as self-loathers because we mask our self-hatred with smiling selfies and positive Instagram posts.

We assign our own self-worth based on what the world deems worthwhile. If we land a great job, our self-esteem soars. But the minute we fail to get that great promotion, our self-image plummets. We fail to realize that the world's changing currency causes great confusion and heartache in the soul of a woman who longs to be loved and valued.

The apostle John writes, "The light shines in the darkness, but the darkness has not understood it" (John 1:5 NIV, 1984). People in Confusedom shift in and out of darkness. We participate in Bible studies, church services, and worship. Maybe we even work at a church or for a ministry. On good days we accept the Truth of God's Word. But on bad days we walk around in a drunken stupor of emotional and spiritual confusion.

In John 1:5 it's almost as if Jesus is telling us, "I'm here. Don't you see Me? I've come to bring hope and order into your chaotic world. I've come to make every wrong in your life right again. I'm standing here in front of you, and yet you still don't see Me. Your darkness is so powerful, so all-consuming, that you continue to choose it over Me."

Isn't that the way it is in our lives sometimes? Jesus stands right before us, ready to walk with us, to live life with us, and yet we turn from Him. We choose our own darkness over His light. Oh, how that must crush His soul.

People in Confusedom look around, whether on social media or in reality (because we all know social media is not reality), and we see people living life seamlessly—the perfect family, the perfect house, the perfect job, the perfect faith—and we wonder, "What am I doing wrong? Why am I not married yet? Why am I not pregnant yet? Why don't I live in my dream home?"

What people in Confusedom don't see underneath those beaming Facebook posts is the crumbling marriage, the house in foreclosure, the credit card debt, and the I'll-show-up-for-church-on-Sunday-morning-but-don't-you-dare-ask-me-do-to-anything-riskier kind of faith.

The apostle John writes, "When Jesus spoke again to the people, he said, 'I am the light of the world. Whoever follows me will never walk in darkness, but will have the light of life'" (John 8:12). Jesus extends the greatest invitation in history to us: "Walk with Me and you will never walk in darkness."

Do you hear Him, friends? Do you hear Him calling to you? He longs for you and for me. He wants nothing more than for you and me to break out of Confusedom and walk with Him in the light. There is no need for us to be confused any longer. We don't need to listen to the voices of the world or the voices in our heads. We don't need to see ourselves through our lens of self-loathing, which causes confusion and bitterness. We need only see ourselves through Jesus' lens of love, which is an invitation to live life in the light. Will you accept His invitation?

Lessons in the Light

Our third and final choice when wallowing in the darkness is to live in the Land of Light. That is my hope for you and for this book—that we will find our way out of the darkness and self-loathing and into the light; that we will stop seeing ourselves as the world sees us, and that we will see ourselves as Jesus sees us, through His lens of love.

If you are reading this book, then you have probably spent too much time entertaining damaging thoughts, engaging in negative self-talk, and participating in emotionally harmful behavior. The time to step out of the darkness and into the light is now. As the apostle Paul writes, "Everything exposed by the light becomes visible—and everything that is illuminated becomes a light. This is why it is said: 'Wake up, sleeper, rise from the dead, and Christ will shine on you'" (Ephesians 5:13–14).

Paul warns us that eventually all sin is exposed. Why not tackle our demons, the things that are eating away at our souls, before we endure any more consequences than we already have? Let us cling to the promise Paul gives us, which is that once we "wake up," "Christ will shine on" us. Who doesn't want the favor of the Savior of the world to rain down on her?

Dr. Martin Luther King Jr. said, "Darkness cannot drive out darkness; only light can do that. Hate cannot drive out hate; only love can do that." We cannot pull ourselves up by our bootstraps, as Americans want to do, and claw our way out of the darkness. If you could, you would not be reading this book. You would have done it years ago. Only by surrendering our thoughts, our words, our choices, and our lives to Jesus can we *drive out* the self-hate and *draw in* Christ's love.

As Jesus Sees. . .You

Self-loathing starts in the mind, flows through the heart, and spills out into our lives. The apostle Paul tells us, "That, however, is not the way of life you learned when you heard about Christ and were taught in him in accordance with the truth that is in Jesus. You were taught, with regard to your former way of life, to put off your old self, which is being corrupted by its deceitful desires; to be made new in the attitude of your minds; and to put on the new self, created to be like God in true righteousness and holiness" (Ephesians 4:20–24). If we want our lives to be filled with love, then we must start by filling our minds with love.

19

Let's play pretend for a moment, shall we? If you could see yourself as Jesus sees you, through His lens of love, how would it change you? Your thought patterns? The way you view yourself?

If you truly stopped thinking about yourself in terms of how you wished you looked or acted, or things you wanted, and then you started seeing yourself from your Savior's point of view, how would you change?

Turn to appendix A, a table titled "As Jesus Sees. . .Me." I filled in the first blank for you. You can fill in the rest. Please take your time on this. It might take you an hour, two hours, two days, or even two weeks. Thoughtfully and prayerfully allow the Holy Spirit to work in you. Don't just *consider* change; *allow change to occur*. Only by seeing the way Jesus sees will we live the way Jesus lived.

As Jesus Sees. . .Your Relationships

If we don't love *ourselves*, we are incapable of loving *others*. So, if you could see yourself as Jesus sees you, through His lens of love, how would it change your relationships? Would you be capable of loving others? Would you be able to achieve more vulnerability with people in your life? Would you be able to form more authentic relationships with others? I think the answer is yes.

When we love ourselves, when we believe we are worthy of love from ourselves, then we open ourselves up to the possibility that we can give love to others and receive it as well.

Some of us, however, have camped out in the darkness so long we don't even know what giving and receiving love looks like. We don't know how to pursue healthy friendships. We haven't dated in a decade. Our marriage has grown stale. How do we even begin to open ourselves up to love? How do we move from self-loathing and contempt to love and affection?

According to Jesus, we extend the same kind of love to others that we want to receive: " 'Love the Lord your God with all your heart and with all your soul and with all your mind.' This is the first and greatest commandment. And the second is like it: 'Love your neighbor as yourself.' All the Law and the Prophets hang on these two commandments'" (Matthew 22:37–40).

Well-known author, speaker, and blogger at Mommastery.com, Glennon Doyle Melton writes, "The Next Right Thing, One Thing At A Time Will Bring You All The Way Home."[1] When we are just beginning to love ourselves and other people, the journey is scary. We don't trust others or ourselves. At every turn we fear pain, betrayal, and loss. Yet if we choose baby steps, if we choose simply to do the next right thing instead of figuring it all out at once, then those little decisions will take us all the way home.

As Jesus Sees. . .Your Community

If you could see as Jesus sees, through His lens of love, how would it change your community—the people you encounter every day? Your neighbor, your coworker, the girl who waits on you at Starbucks every morning. When we wrap ourselves in self-loathing, when we drown ourselves in the darkness, there is no room to minister to others in the light.

Dr. Martin Luther King Jr. said, "I have decided to stick with love. Hate is too great a burden to bear." Wouldn't it feel refreshing, life giving, to brush off that burden and choose love? Don't you want to run out of the darkness, and into the light, not only for yourself, but for all those people you know are counting on you? They are waiting for you, friend. Let's not keep them waiting any longer.

If we are going to see as Jesus sees, we must exchange self-loathing for love. The apostle John writes of Jesus' steadfast love: "It was just before the Passover Festival. Jesus knew that the hour had come for him to leave this world and go to the Father. Having loved his own who were in the world, he loved them to the end" (John 13:1). The trick is that, like Jesus, we must love everyone, including ourselves, "to the end." The journey never stops. We don't get a day off. We can't call in sick.

We must love even when we don't feel like it. We must love on the easy days and on the difficult days. We must love until our Savior returns or calls us home. . .and then we must love some more.

As Jesus Sees. . .Your Relationship with God

One of the most quoted Bible verses of our time is John 3:16. We learn it in Sunday school, read it in books, and even see it on posters in the stands at football games: "For God so loved the world that he gave his one and only Son, that whoever believes in him shall not perish but have eternal life" (John 3:16). It leads me to ask this question: If you could see as Jesus sees, through His lens of love, how would it change your relationship with your Creator? Do you believe God loves you? Do you believe He loves you so deeply, so passionately, so radically that He watched His one and only Son die a horrific death at the hands of unjustified people, all so that you could live for eternity with Him in heaven?

If you could see as Jesus sees, through His lens of love, then you would see how much His Father—God the Father—loves you. You would see how much God gave up for you and how much He loves you.

Take a few moments now and use the space below to journal about how much God loves you. Try seeing yourself from your Creator's perspective and keep in mind John 3:16 as you write.

_____

_____

_____

_____

_____

_____

Future Lens

So why are we focusing so much on our lens of self-loathing? Seems like a downer chapter to start with, right? Because all other topics, all other chapters, flow from this lens. If we see ourselves through a lens of self-loathing, then we most likely see ourselves through these lenses as well:

- a lens of ugliness
- a lens of shame
- a lens of incompetence
- a lens of inadequacy
- a lens of isolation
- a lens of greed
- a lens of burden
- a lens of fear
- a lens of unforgiveness

Yet if we switch our lens and see ourselves as Jesus sees, then we will soon see ourselves through these lenses:

- a lens of beauty
- a lens of redemption
- a lens of talent
- a lens of acceptance
- a lens of belonging
- a lens of generosity
- a lens of blessing
- a lens of bravery
- a lens of forgiveness

We must begin tackling our feelings of self-loathing if we are to move forward into these other areas of our mental, emotional, physical, and spiritual health. It might seem daunting—an uphill climb too steep for even the most seasoned athlete. But rest assured, you can do it! We are climbing this mountain together, and we will not stop until we are at the top.

Personal Reflection Questions

1. In the beginning of chapter 1, Elizabeth describes the first time she remembers experiencing feelings of self-loathing. Do you recall when you had your first negative thought about yourself? If so, describe it here.

    - How old were you?
    - What were the circumstances?
    - How did you feel and think?
    - Did you tell someone, or did you suffer in silence?
    - How did your friends and family react?
    - What was the outcome?

    _____

    _____

    _____

    _____

    _____

2. If you currently struggle with self-loathing, does it stem from your own sin or sins committed against you? Explain.

    _____

    _____

    _____

    _____

    _____

3. Elizabeth explains three ways in which we handle self-loathing: by living in Stucksville, Confusedom, or the Land of Light.

- In which place have you lived most of your life?
- In which place do you find yourself today?
- Where do you want to go? Are you ready to make that commitment? If so, write a prayer to God committing yourself to the process, no matter how emotionally and spiritually painful it might be. Then ask Him for the strength to see you through to the end.

_____

_____

_____

_____

_____

4. If you could see as Jesus sees, through His lens of love, how would it affect the way you view yourself?

- Would you see yourself as worthy of love? Why or why not?
- What would "loving yourself" look like in a practical, everyday way?

_____

_____

_____

_____

5. If you could see as Jesus sees, through His lens of love, how would it affect your relationships?

- Would you see yourself as capable of loving others? Explain.
- Is there someone specific whom God is calling you to become more vulnerable with in your life? If so, explain.
- Would you be able to form more authentic relationships with others? Explain what that looks like in a practical sense.

_____

_____

_____

_____

_____

_____

_____

_____

_____

_____

_____

_____

_____

Group Reflection Questions

1. What appealed to you about this study?

2. What made you want to do it in a group setting as opposed to on your own?

3. How would you sum up your thoughts about chapter 1 in one or two sentences?

4. In the beginning of chapter 1, Elizabeth describes the first time she remembers experiencing feelings of self-loathing. Do you recall the time when you had your first negative thought about yourself? If so, describe it here.

    - How old were you?
    - What were the circumstances?
    - How did you feel and think?
    - Did you suffer in silence?
    - How did your friends and family react?
    - What was the outcome?

5. Elizabeth explains three ways in which we handle our self-loathing: by living in Stucksville, Confusedom, or the Land of Light.

    - In which place have you lived most of your life?
    - In which place do you find yourself today?
    - Where do you want to go?

6. In the Personal Reflection Questions, you were asked to define what it meant to see yourself as "worthy of love." What did you come up with?

7. If you could see as Jesus sees, through His lens of love, how could you go about forming more authentic relationships with others?

8. If you could see as Jesus sees, through His lens of love, in what practical ways could you engage in your community in a different, more meaningful way from what you currently are doing?

9. In the last part of this chapter, the "Future Lens," Elizabeth lists all the ways in which looking through a lens of self-loathing affects our lives. Which of these struck a chord with you?

10. Overall, what do you hope to get out of this study?

Chapter 2

My Lens of Ugliness, His Lens of Beauty

Women are strange creatures. We sit around comparing and contrasting different body parts with one another as if this body bashing will somehow result in a magical transformation.

"You're so much skinnier than me."

"Whatever. You got the good hair. It's so much thicker than mine."

"Yeah, but you have the rockin' booty. I go to boot camp three times a week, and I still don't look like Beyoncé."

"Stop whining. I'd kill to have your abs. I do crunches every night, and my tummy always looks like I'm three months postpartum." The list goes on and on and on.

Back to the movie *Mean Girls*. (Can you tell I really like this movie? I'm a sucker for anything Tina Fey.) In one particular scene, Lindsay Lohan, who plays Cady Heron, a homeschooled student transplanted from Africa to the United States, realizes this wicked game American girls play with one another. She watches with a bewildered look on her face as her friends, aka "the Plastics," tear themselves apart in the mirror.

"My hips are huge!"

"Oh, please. I hate my calves."

"At least you girls can wear halters. I've got man shoulders."

Cady hesitantly walks toward her frenemies while the monologue running through her head quips, *I used to think there was just fat or skinny, but apparently there's a lot of things that can be wrong on your body.*

So it seems, Cady. So it seems.

Elizabeth Oates

The Media

It's no secret that the media is not our friend when it comes to our self-esteem. So why do we continue buying into its lies? We know magazines airbrush their cover girls. We know models require a team of makeup artists, hairstylists, clothing designers, and lighting technicians before that perfect shot is snapped. And don't forget the eager intern waiting in the wings with a fan. I don't have an intern, but I do have four kids; maybe I should pay them a quarter to chase me around with a fan. At least then I might *feel* like a supermodel.

Intellectually we know this media game is all superficial hype designed to create a greater chasm between the haves and the have-nots. The entertainment and fashion industries tempt us have-nots into wanting and buying—even though we cannot afford—whatever they are selling. The models, designers, and fashion mogul marketing geniuses don their Michael Kors, Jimmy Choo, and Prada while we sport our Old Navy threads—and our self-esteem plummets.

Don't even get me started on our bodies. Diets are now starting as young as kindergarten while eating disorders and body dysmorphia are thriving in our culture. Rader Programs reported the results of a number of studies that give evidence of women's dissatisfaction with their body image:

- One study showed that women experience an average of 13 negative thoughts about their bodies each day, while 97 percent of women admit to having at least one "I hate my body" moment each day.
- One study showed that 75 percent of the women surveyed considered themselves overweight when, in reality, only 25 percent were.
- A *Glamour* magazine survey showed that 61 percent of respondents felt ashamed of their hips, 64 percent felt embarrassed by their stomachs, and 72 percent were ashamed of their thighs.
- Four out of five women in the United States are unhappy with their appearance.

- The average US model weighs 117 pounds and is 5 feet 11 inches, while the average US woman weighs 140 pounds and is 5 feet 4 inches.
- A *People* magazine survey showed that 80 percent of female respondents admitted that women in movies and television programs made them feel insecure about their bodies.[1]

A Moving Target

The thing about beauty is that the standard changes. When I was in college, everyone plucked their eyebrows. So, in the spirit of accountability, my roommates taught me how to pluck my own brows. I plucked so much you would have thought I worked on a chicken farm.

Fast-forward fifteen years. Thin eyebrows are no longer in style—which is unfortunate, because my eyebrows have never fully grown back. So now I have a drawer stocked with brown eyebrow liner. *Sigh.*

Beauty is also subjective. Growing up I never liked my nose. It had a bump on it—big deal. But in my mind, little bump = big nose. People always said I looked like Barbra Streisand, Jennifer Grey (*Dirty Dancing*), or Mayim Bialik (star of the 1990s hit *Blossom*, for all those gen Xers, or *The Big Bang Theory*, for the millennials). I hated my big nose and made big plans to get a big nose job.

Be careful what you wish for. During a college trip to Costa Rica to study Spanish, I was assaulted and robbed by four local guys. I immediately returned home to the States with a black eye and, you guessed it, a broken nose. Nothing a simple nose surgery wouldn't fix.

Ironically, I always thought getting a nose job would solve all my beauty woes. A nose job would make me look ten pounds lighter and a hundred times prettier. A nose job would lift my spirits and make my life all around happier. Except that it didn't. After that momentous nose job, for which I had waited my entire life (okay, all twenty-two years), I didn't feel lighter or prettier or happier. I didn't feel any different at all. I was just the same girl with a slightly different nose. Big letdown.

And that nose that I spent so many years hating? In retrospect, it didn't seem so ugly or big. I remember a few years after my nose job, I sat watching an entertainment news show and the anchor reported on a young starlet who also got a nose job. "She was beautiful before her nose job," the anchor said. "I wish she hadn't gotten the bump taken off. It was so cute."

"*What?*" I wanted to turn my newly crafted nose up at her. "What do you mean her old nose was cute?" And then I realized something: the anchor was right. The actress's nose *was* cute before her surgery. Why hadn't anyone ever told me *my* nose was cute? Or had they? Maybe I never listened. Knowing my stubborn nature, that was quite possible. I continued to mull it over, for the first time in my life missing my old nose.

Beauty is a moving target. God's Word and truth are constant. If we don't stay focused on the only fixed standard—Jesus—we will get distracted.

Keep It in Perspective

We might disagree about our bodies, our eyebrows, or our noses, but I think the one thing we can agree on is feet. Feet are gross. It's a fact. Unless you are a six-month-old baby, feet are ugly. In the fifth grade, I refused to wear sandals or flip-flops for a year because I hated my feet (really I should have been embarrassed by my bad perm and 1980s fashion, but whatever).

Yes, feet are unpleasant. I know Jesus is the Son of God, but I have a feeling even His feet were unattractive. And stinky. And gross. After a day of walking around in a town with no sewage system and lots of animal feces, dirt, and garbage lining the streets, it's safe to say Jesus' sandals needed some Odor-Eaters. So it's hard for me to cast stones at Simon, who turned up his nose (probably literally) at Jesus' feet when He walked in the house.

"Then [Jesus] turned toward the woman and said to Simon, 'Do you see this woman? I came into your house. You did not give me any water for my feet, but she wet my feet with her tears and wiped them with her hair. You did not give me a kiss, but this woman, from the time I entered, has not stopped kissing my feet. You did not put oil on my head, but she has poured perfume on my feet'" (Luke 7:44–46).

Simon refused to tend to Jesus' feet. But not "this woman." Nope. The unnamed woman not only washed Jesus' feet, she used her hair—her *hair*! The most beautiful, glorious, valuable part of a woman's body in Jesus' day! Now, I don't have much hair (it's my second biggest insecurity after my nose, so now you know all my secrets), so I can't even imagine the sacrifice. But I'm guessing this woman had thick, wavy, luscious locks of dark, coarse, Middle Eastern hair—the perfect texture for wiping camel dung off the Son of God's toes.

When we take a step back, the entire scene is like walking into a fun house where everything is turned upside down. How could this unnamed woman use her beauty and her "glory" to wipe away something so disgusting and offensive? Because in this fun house, the unnamed woman kept her beauty in perspective.

What Simon saw as disdainful—Jesus' feet—the woman saw as worthy of honor. Yes, she knew her hair was beautiful, but she also knew that beauty was not something to keep for herself; it was not something to hoard or hold in higher regard than the King. It was something to cherish and to be shared with the King. Her hair, her beauty, was not something *to* worship; rather, it was something to use *for* worship.

What the world saw as inferior—the unnamed woman—Jesus saw as beautiful. We do not know this woman's name, which leads us to believe not many other people knew it either. She wasn't important enough, not prominent enough, to merit a name. My guess is that few noticed her slip into Simon's house. . .until Jesus noticed her.

Did you know:

- Only 2 percent of women think they are beautiful.[2]
- Sixty percent of women eighteen years and older are in favor of plastic surgery.[3]
- Between 1997 and 2013, the number of plastic surgery procedures for women increased over 471 percent.[4]
- In 2013, liposuction replaced breast augmentation as the most popular cosmetic surgery procedure for women, with a 16 percent increase and more than a billion dollars spent on the procedure.[5]

Our perspective on elegance, artistry, and charm changes every few years as the world tells us what is "in" and what is "out." Our outlook on style has become so skewed that we hardly recognize true beauty anymore. We see through the lens of broken, lost people desperately trying to convince ourselves of what is beautiful. So we look. And we look. And we look some more. We trust other flawed people to determine our standard of beauty because we stopped seeing the world through Jesus' lens.

Defining True Beauty

Beauty is not *what* we look like, but *who* we look like. The more we look like Jesus, the more beautiful we are.

If you have given birth, then you know what an awe-inspiring journey it is to carry a tiny human in your belly for nine months then usher her or him into the world and watch that newborn gasp for air for the very first time. There is no other miracle like it on earth (that is, of course, if you can make it past the first nine months of morning sickness, heartburn, back pain, and insomnia).

If you have adopted a child, then you understand the wonder of another woman entrusting her child—her very flesh and blood—to you. You understand the sacrifice, the pain, and the gift. Currently I am mothering my three biological children and a foster child, and I am reminded every day that, yes, some children come to us from our wombs and some children come to us from an agency, but all children come from God. And they all are incredible little people.

These tiny humans wreak havoc on our bodies in many ways: stretch marks, tummy pooches, love handles, acne, wrinkles, bags under our eyes, gray hairs, and tears of joy and stress. Yet children also bless us in ways we often overlook. They can be funny and generous and quick to forgive—much more so than their jaded parents. Without knowing it, they offer their mothers a lifetime of unconditional love, refinement, and purpose. And for that I am forever grateful.

If you have not or cannot bear children, your body is just as miraculous. You have lungs that breathe. You have legs that run. You have arms that hug and provide empathy for those who need compassion. You have a heart that beats and provides friendship for those who feel minute and alone in this great big world. You have a brain that computes the words on these pages, and you have the awesome power to decide to change your life and see yourself as Jesus sees you—as beautiful and glorious and magnificent. Or you can stay exactly where you are and see yourself exactly as you have always seen yourself—as ugly, unpleasant, and plain.

Think back to a moment in time when you yourself were a tiny human. Maybe you were four, five, or even six years old. Maybe you took gymnastics or dance or scored the winning goal on the soccer field. What were you wearing? How was your hair fixed? Try to get in your own headspace. Close your eyes for a moment if you must.

Now, think about how you felt. Did you feel pretty? Cute? Confident? Strong? Did thoughts about beauty, weight, height, or bone structure even occur to you? Or was it enough for you just to breathe? It's been a long time since the world gave us permission to merely exist.

This, my friend, is where we begin to define true beauty: at the place where we first learn to exist and breathe. This is the place where we pause, we reflect, and we believe that maybe God got it right after all. Maybe our appearance is exactly as it should be. Maybe we are not too short or too wide or too lanky or too freckly or too dark or too light or too bulky or too frail. This is the moment when we fully accept and embrace ourselves. Just as a mother loves her newborn baby, we love every square inch of ourselves. Why? Because we are the exact design God wanted according to His plan and purpose. We are perfectly flawed, yet perfectly beautiful.

I remember that when my first son was born, I told my husband, "I know all moms think their babies are the cutest, but Carter really *is* the cutest." Even after all the good hospital drugs wore off, I believed it. I believed with every fiber of my soul that *my* son was the cutest baby on the planet. I also believed that every other mother believed her baby was the cutest, but I knew they were all delusional and Carter was the winner in my self-imposed baby pageant.

Just as a mother dotes on her newborn baby's pink, wrinkly, soft, squishy flesh, God delights in us. Just as a mother knows her infant is the most beautiful snuggle bug in the world, God knows you are the most beautiful, radiant, flawless creature He has ever created.

Do you believe God is a truth teller? Or do you believe God is a liar? If you believe God is truthful, then you must believe Him when He says you are beautiful. Why? Because the Bible tells us we are "wonderfully made" unique creations.

Psalm 139:13–16 reads:

> *You created my inmost being; you knit me together in my mother's womb. I praise you because I am fearfully and wonderfully made; your works are wonderful, I know that full well. My frame was not hidden from you when I was made in the secret place, when I was woven together in the depths of the earth. Your eyes saw my unformed body; all the days ordained for me were written in your book before one of them came to be.*

Every time someone—whether our husband, our friend, or our parent—gives us a compliment and we turn it down, we call that person a liar. Every time we criticize ourselves, we call God a liar.

Fifteen years and four children later, I have a new perspective on that coveted nose job—and plastic surgery in general. Someday, one (if not all three) of my biological children will complain about their big noses. Right now they all have cute, little noses; but one day the big nose will appear along with acne, puberty, and periods. Good times. Can't wait.

I will tell my kids their noses are cute and perfect just the way God made them. And fifteen years after altering my own my nose, I believe these words. Why? Because I now see myself and my children through Jesus' lens of beauty. Where we see ugliness, Jesus sees beauty. If God created the stars and the planets and the heavens and the earth, can we not trust Him to perfectly handcraft us as well?

Living Out Our Beauty

Beauty is not what we do but who we do it for. True beauty comes from living out our faith and living out the plans God has for us. According to Jeremiah 29:11, God created each of us with a plan in mind: "'For I know the plans I have for you,' declares the LORD, 'plans to prosper you and not to harm you, plans to give you hope and a future.'"

God had a plan for the unnamed woman when He created her with thick, dark hair. He knew that one day that hair would be used for more than just head adornment; it would be used to wipe His Son's feet. She was courageous enough to live out this plan. When she saw Jesus' feet, she didn't see dirt; she saw the hundreds of miles He walked to do the work of His Father. When she poured perfume on Jesus' feet, she didn't smell the putrid stench of animal feces; she smelled the sweet aroma of salvation. When she wiped His feet with her hair, she didn't feel the wet, sticky sewage; she felt God in the flesh. What I love about this unnamed woman is that she didn't see the world the way Simon saw the world—or the way you and I see the world. She saw the world, she saw Jesus, and she saw herself through a lens of beauty. Just as God had a plan for the unnamed woman, He has a purpose for you, too. This purpose encompasses your appearance, your personality, your giftedness, and your talents.

Every day I watch some of the most talented people living on mission. My friends Brett and Emily Mills, musicians and cofounders of a nonprofit called Jesus Said Love, fiercely love others so that the Gospel can be taken into exotic dance clubs across Texas and women can feel loved and accepted in the name of Jesus.

I listen to other foster moms exchange stories of broken children entering their families and their homes only to walk out again with shattered hopes and dreams. Yet these mothers continue to juggle their husbands, their biological children, and their jobs, all while loving these desperate children with reckless abandon.

I talk to teachers for whom prepping students for state-mandated tests are not the end goal; rather, loving our children well and raising a generation of humans filled with compassion and integrity is their ultimate finish line.

I watch moms caring selflessly for their sick children. I see dads working tirelessly to provide for their families. I notice pastors leading and challenging their flocks to live beyond the American dream.

I see people every day living with humility and kindness and bravery and generosity and hospitality. No books will be written about them. No songs sung. No stories told. Yet they are impacting lives nonetheless. Their beauty comes not from the makeup they wear or the size of their clothes, but from the way they treat people and how they live their lives. They exude joy and radiate love.

Banish the Negative Self-Talk

Bestselling author and contributor for the *Huffington Post*, Jillian Lauren, wrote:

> *Last week, I sat down in a Macy's dressing room and cried because I was so desperately sick of hating myself. I can't remember a time I didn't feel like someone made a mistake when they made me—the wrong shape, the wrong size, clumsy, thick. . . This bizarrely distorted lens is reserved for use only on myself. When it comes to other people, I have an expansive view of beauty, both physical and not. The self-hatred isn't constant, but it is always lying in wait for a window of opportunity. I can be going along my merry self-accepting way when a moment of social anxiety, a rejection or even just a hard morning will trigger a full-force flood of poison, and the conclusion is always this: I am so ugly that I don't deserve to be alive.[6]*

Do you ever have moments like this? Where you hate yourself so much you'd rather not even be alive? It takes a lot of negative self-talk to arrive at this point, but unfortunately, more women pull into that station than we care to admit.

Think about the negative self-talk you feed yourself on a regular basis. Things like this:

- My ears stick out.
- I need to lose ten pounds.
- I hate my thighs.

Now that we have defined true beauty, it's time to banish the negative self-talk. Find a piece of paper and write down all of the negative things you say to yourself. One at a time. Every single thing. Write down every negative thing you say to yourself every day. Go ahead. I'll wait.

Let's try another exercise. Look at your list again. This time cross out the words "my" or "I" and insert your friends' names. For example:

- My hips are too wide.

  ~~My~~ Stacey, your hips are too wide.
- My thighs are too flabby.

  ~~My~~ Rachael, your thighs are too flabby.
- My hair is too frizzy.

  ~~My~~ Mandy, your hair is too frizzy.

Do you hear how cruel (and ridiculous) you sound? We would never in a million years say to our friends the things we say to ourselves. If we did, we would spend a lot more nights sitting on the couch watching *The Bachelor* all by ourselves instead of hanging out with friends.

Worse yet, if you are a mother, can you imagine speaking to your daughter the way you speak to yourself? This kind of negative talk would damage her psyche and take years, if not the rest of her life, to recover from.

Do you realize that every time we criticize our appearance, we criticize our Creator? Every time we complain about our hair, we tell the One who made our hair that He didn't do a very good job. Every time we whine about our thighs, we tell the One who handcrafted our legs that He should have made them longer, leaner, or more muscular. He made a mistake. He didn't know what He was doing. We know better.

Would you ever criticize Picasso? Would you have the audacity to pick apart his work? You would be foolish to do so. He was a master artist with more credibility than you. You barely passed fourth-grade art. (Okay, maybe that's me.)

Jesus would never look at us through a lens of ugliness and distaste. So why do we look at ourselves this way? Because we have spent years seeing ourselves through the world's eyes instead of through the eyes of the One who created us. And why do we spend our lives trying to please those whom we will never please, when the One who created us is pleased with us just the way we are?

As Jesus Sees. . .You

I recently talked with a friend, Martha Kate, who battled anorexia for twelve years. Martha Kate is compassionate, brave, and kind; and most importantly, she is a survivor.

"The first time I became conscious of my body, I was three years old. I was taught what a diet was and how to do it. I was taught we could control how we looked. When I was five I was called 'fat' on the playground. From then on I was very conscious of how I looked and how other people looked," remembers Martha Kate. "In the fifth grade, I began controlling what went in and out of my body. From age ten until my junior year in college, I battled with food and exercise and restricted what I ate.

"During those twelve years of battling anorexia, there was lots of negative self-talk and lies. I basically had a tape of lies playing on repeat in my head: 'You're ugly. You're not worth it. You're not pretty enough. You're not thin enough.' All that negative self-talk affected how I ate, what I ate, how I exercised, what I wore, how I did my makeup, who I interacted with, how I interacted with them. It affected how I lived my life," she recalls.

Fortunately for Martha Kate, she knew her eating disorder had a tight grip on her, and she eventually sought therapy. "I joined RUF [Reformed University Fellowship] and heard this sermon, and it just clicked how Jesus loved broken people. I had always thought that meant other people. But I finally realized Jesus loved *me* even though *I* was messy and broken.

"Someone once told me, 'It's okay that you're not okay, because Jesus is better than being you being better than everyone else.' That became my motto. I don't have to be pretty enough or thin enough. Jesus is enough for me. From that moment on, I embraced grace. Things changed in my head. It wasn't an overnight process, but slowly I was able to embrace grace and leave my eating disorder behind. And once I understood the Gospel was about grace and Jesus was about grace, it was okay if I messed up. It was okay if I wasn't perfect, because

Jesus paid it all, and my works and my striving to be perfect didn't add anything to what Jesus did on the cross."

Can you relate to Martha Kate's story? Can you relate to her struggle to see herself as Jesus sees, through His lens of beauty? Once she did, she experienced such grace and freedom. If you could see as Jesus sees, through His lens of beauty, how would it change you? How would it affect your self-image? Would you spend less time in the gym and more time in prayer? Would you spend less time in front of the mirror and more time reflecting on His Word?

Now that we have discussed what beauty is not and we have defined what true beauty is, take a few moments to write down what your life would look like if you could truly embrace God's view of your internal and external beauty. (Use the few questions above to get you started.)

As Jesus Sees. . .Your Relationships

Someone once told me, "Treat every person you meet not as a stranger, but as a soul." If we neglect our own souls, how can we nourish someone else's? If we are not treating ourselves with kindness and compassion, how can we extend empathy to someone else?

When we criticize ourselves, we belittle others. When we focus on our flaws, we see the weaknesses in others. However, if you could see as Jesus sees, through His lens of beauty, how would this affect your relationships? Could you peer into your sister's heart and find her inner beauty instead of focusing on her outer shell? Could you appreciate your colleague's work ethic instead of berating her shortcomings?

Scripture tells us that the world will know we follow Jesus Christ by the way we treat others: "By this everyone will know that you are my disciples, if you love one another" (John 13:35).

Think of the tidal wave of change that could occur if we channeled all our beauty-focused energy into loving and supporting one another. Take some time to write down any people in whom God is calling you to find true beauty. Ready. Set. Go be that tidal wave.

As Jesus Sees. . .Your Community

At a recent Bible study, a friend said that we are called to live out our purpose right where we are. Then she posed this question: "Where are you every day? Are you at the grocery store? Are you at work? Are you at home?" Wherever you are on a daily basis, that's your community. Those are your people. You might not know them intimately, but that girl who bags your groceries every day needs to know she is beautiful. Your three-your-old daughter needs to know she is precious. Your mother who is dying of cancer needs to know she is radiant. Yet how can we look these women in the eye and convince them of their own beauty if we don't accept the truth that God created us with this same inner and outer beauty?

If you could see as Jesus sees, through His lens of beauty, how would it affect your community? Based on our definition of true beauty and knowing how we can live out our beauty, how would you be able to minister to those whom you encounter on a daily basis? Take a moment to answer this question in the space provided.

_____

_____

_____

_____

_____

_____

_____

_____

_____

_____

Elizabeth Oates

As Jesus Sees. . .Your Relationship with God

During a tornado warning, while most of our friends were hunkered down in hallways and pantries and bathrooms, we took our chances and watched the movie *Heaven Is for Real* with our children.

In between all the complaining—"This is boring" and "This is creepy"—we actually enjoyed it. Making memories, I tell ya.

My favorite part of the movie is when the little boy, Colton, is in heaven and Jesus approaches him and takes his hand. For just a split second, I tried to imagine what that moment will be like when the Savior of the world, who died for you and for me, walks up to me, looks me in the eyes, and takes my hand. I could hardly catch my breath.

King Solomon wrote to his bride, "You are altogether beautiful, my darling; there is no flaw in you" (Song of Songs 4:7). I think Jesus would say the same thing about us. There is no flaw in us because God created us. So let me tell you, friend, you are altogether beautiful. There is no flaw in you.

If you could see as Jesus sees, through His lens of beauty, how would it change your relationship with your Creator? Using this verse or any other part of the chapter as your guide, take some time to journal your thoughts.

_____

_____

_____

_____

_____

_____

_____

Personal Reflection Questions

1. How has the media affected your self-esteem?

   • Give some examples of movies, TV shows, or magazines that have affected your self-esteem either positively or negatively.

   _____

   _____

   _____

2. Elizabeth talks about the standard of beauty being a moving target. Do you agree or disagree with this statement?

   • How has this played out in your own life?

   _____

   _____

   _____

   _____

3. We all know plastic surgery is a hot topic in our culture, and even Elizabeth confesses to having had a nose job. What are your feelings about plastic surgery?

   • Do you think plastic surgery honors or dishonors God?
   • Have you ever had plastic surgery? If so, do you regret it, or are you glad you did it?
   • If you chose plastic surgery and regret it, pray to

God. Let Him know you are ready to find your self-confidence in Him and through His lens of beauty.

_____

_____

_____

_____

_____

_____

4. Take some time to look up Psalm 139:13–16 in at least two Bible translations other than the NIV.

    • What did you learn from looking up these verses in different translations?
    • What did you like about the different translations?
    • What was your favorite translation? Why?

_____

_____

_____

_____

_____

_____

5. Elizabeth writes, "If God created the stars and the planets and the heavens and the earth, can we not trust Him to perfectly handcraft us as well?"

    - Do you agree or disagree?
    - Can you back this statement up with scripture?
    - If you agree, how can you apply this to your own life and begin seeing yourself through Jesus' lens of beauty?

    _____

    _____

    _____

    _____

    _____

    _____

    _____

    _____

    _____

    _____

    _____

    _____

    _____

    _____

Group Reflection Questions

1. How has the media affected your self-esteem?

   - Give some examples of movies, TV shows, or magazines that have affected your self-esteem either positively or negatively.

2. Elizabeth talks about the standard of beauty being a moving target. Do you agree or disagree with this statement?

   - How has this played out in your own life?

3. Compare Simon's response to Jesus with the unnamed woman's response to Jesus.

   - Why was it such a big deal that she used her hair to wash Jesus' feet?
   - How do you think you would have reacted in this situation?

4. Elizabeth writes, "If God created the stars and the planets and the heavens and the earth, can we not trust Him to perfectly handcraft us as well?"

   - Do you agree or disagree?
   - Can you back this statement up with scripture?
   - If you agree, how can you apply this to your own life and begin seeing yourself through Jesus' lens of beauty?

5. Elizabeth cites the statistic, "Only 2 percent of women think they are beautiful."

    • Given the women in your own community/sphere of influence, do you think this statistic is accurate? Why or why not?

6. Did you engage in the "Banish the Negative Self-Talk" exercise?

    • How did it go?
    • Was it difficult to do?
    • What surprised you about it?

7. What truth resonated most with you this week?

Chapter 3

My Lens of Shame, His Lens of Redemption

Author, speaker, and professor, Brené Brown, has spent over a decade studying shame. "At its core," Brown says, "shame is the intensely painful feeling or experience of believing that we are flawed and therefore unworthy of love and belonging."[1]

The fact is, we all are flawed. Every single one of us. We exit our mother's womb broken, damaged goods in need of a Savior to repair and restore us. Paul writes to the Romans, "For all have sinned and fall short of the glory of God" (Romans 3:23). Not one of us is excluded from this category. The question then becomes, will we allow Jesus into the darkest places of our soul to redeem us? Or will we withdraw, crawling into the recesses of our minds far away from anyone who can help us, and live a life of shame and deterioration?

Brown continues, "We're afraid that people won't like us if they know the truth about who we are, where we come from, what we believe, how much we're struggling, or, believe it or not, how wonderful we are when soaring."[2]

Isn't that what social media is all about these days? Hiding our true selves for fear people discover and develop a disdain for us? So we play a part, a role in life. We put on a façade out of fear. *What if they find out that underneath my smile lies a deep layer of depression? What if they discover my marriage is only one step away from divorce? What if they realize my religious views rub against my political views? What if they find out my child is struggling in school? Or worse, what if they see I am actually succeeding, yet my success comes at a high price?* We fear all of these things, and when we succumb to our fears, we feel shame. "We tend to associate shame with a major trauma or a defining negative event—an abusive childhood, a painful addiction, a seemingly intractable pile of credit card debt—but the experience of feeling unworthy is universal, no matter what hides out in our past. Everyone, save for sociopaths, experiences some degree of shame. This messy emotion turns up in the most 'familiar places, including appearance and body image, family, parenting, money and work, health, addiction, sex, aging, and religion,' writes [Brené] Brown. 'To feel shame is to be human.'"[3]

Like self-loathing, I would say almost every woman feels shame at some point, to some degree. The dictionary definition of shame is "the painful feeling arising from the consciousness of something dishonorable, improper, ridiculous, etc., done by oneself or another."[4] Who hasn't done something dishonorable, improper, or at least ridiculous at some point in her life?

Unfortunately, not a day goes by that I don't lie in bed wishing I had:

- spoken to my children more gently
- thought before sending a text message in haste
- been more encouraging and less defensive
- been more of a giver and less of a taker
- responded more calmly in a group e-mail
- spent more time playing with my children and less time checking Instagram
- prayed more and worried less
- checked up on a friend
- encouraged my husband more

And the list goes on. The point is that I end every day full of shame for opportunities missed and consequences suffered.

One area in which I struggle is the stay-at-home mom versus working mom debate. Currently I am a stay-at-home mom, but I do some freelance writing and teach a few yoga classes during the week. If you ask my children, they will quickly tell you that I don't have a "real job." *Ouch.* I guess I will remind them of that the next time they want breakfast. "Sorry, kids, it's not in my 'fake job' description."

Many days I feel ashamed that I loathe the endless days of Play-Doh, playdates, and playing pretend. I am not wired for this. I am an ESTJ (that's "extroverted, sensing, thinking, judging" for all you non-Myers-Briggs junkies). My celebrity ESTJ persona is Darth Vader—*Darth Vader*! Would you want Darth Vader raising your children? Me neither. I am pretty ill equipped for this preschool stage, and yet, by the grace of God, my kids have escaped their toddler years relatively unscathed. Hallelujah! Must be all that Noggin and Nick Jr. I let them watch—"It's like preschool on TV."

I long for a career, a real get-dressed-and-go-to-the-office-with-real-responsibilities-and-a-paycheck career. Yet I know this is the place God has me, at least for now. Some days my husband takes the kids so I can spend an afternoon writing, and I miss out on family time. Again, I feel ashamed—ashamed that I am not spending time with my family. So whether I am with my kids or away from them, I feel some sort of shame and guilt because I am not living up to some picture-perfect ideal I have painted in my head. And the shame cycle continues.

Women are masters at carrying guilt that was never intended for us—am I right? If I could see as Jesus sees, then I would cast aside any ounce of shame and see myself through His lens of redemption. I would realize God has me exactly where He wants me at this season in my life, however excruciating or precious that might be at any given moment. It is only when I shift my perspective and view my life through the world's lens telling me to "be more important," "do something more significant," "achieve something greater" that I succumb to those feelings of shame.

What are some other areas that bring shame to women of our generation? The list is long. Probably too long. We feel shame for things both big and small, both past and present, both within and beyond our control. Below are some areas that might resonate with you. (Please note, I am not saying we *should* feel shame for the things on this list, I am simply saying we *tend* to feel shame for the things on this list, plus many more.) Pause for a few minutes to read through the list, and then add to it. Maybe even call a few friends, your sister, your cousin, or your neighbor to get their perspectives. Feel free to continue adding to this list as you work through the chapter.

Things that cause us to feel shame:

- pride
- missed opportunities
- poor choices
- sexual impurity
- eating disorders
- sexual abuse / sexual assault
- addictions
- family dysfunction
- failure
- socioeconomic status

Do you identify with anything on that list? If so, read the following verse: "Therefore, if anyone is in Christ, the new creation has come: The old has gone, the new is here!" (2 Corinthians 5:17) That is reason to celebrate, my friend! If you know Jesus Christ as your Savior, then you are no longer the woman condemned and sentenced to carry your shame until you take your last breath. God sent His only Son to earth to live and die for you. That day on the cross, God made a monumental trade never before accomplished and never again repeated in history: God exchanged our shame for His redemption. You and I were set free!

So why do we still allow our shame to suffocate us?

Hide-and-Seek

In chapter 1 we talked a lot about not wallowing in the darkness—or self-loathing—but choosing instead to live in the light. Like self-loathing, shame is also a place of darkness, secrecy, and silence. How many of us have been playing hide-and-seek the majority of our lives? How many of us have lived in secrecy and silence, fearful of the aftermath if the source of our shame is exposed?

And yet, ironically, concealment is the very thing that fuels our shame. So we continue to withdraw. We distance ourselves from our friends and family. We pull out of our favorite activities, hobbies, and clubs, or we never get involved in the first place.

If we want to rid our lives of shame, we must step out of the darkness and step into the light. We must unleash the past and give a voice to our shame.

Scripture tells us that "if we walk in the light, as he is in the light, we have fellowship with one another, and the blood of Jesus, his Son, purifies us from all sin" (1 John 1:7). John asserts that true emotional and spiritual healing is rarely accomplished solo. We must walk with Jesus and in fellowship with other believers if we want to overcome our demons and live in the light.

Even Jesus walked with a group of close friends: Peter, James, and John. These men were human, flawed, and even disappointing at times, yet Jesus trusted and loved them. They were His inner circle, three men set apart from the rest of the disciples, whom He taught and shaped and with whom He traveled. Scripture tells us that Jesus shared glorious moments, such as His transfiguration, with these friends. Yet He also leaned on them at one of the most difficult times in His life and ministry:

> *He took Peter, James, and John with Him; and as they left the larger group behind, He became distressed and filled with sorrow.*

Jesus: My heart is so heavy; I feel as if I could die. Wait here for Me, and stay awake to keep watch.

He walked on a little farther. Then He threw Himself on the ground and prayed for deliverance from what was about to come.

Jesus: Abba, Father, I know that anything is possible for You. Please take this cup away so I don't have to drink from it. But whatever happens, let Your will be done—not Mine.

He got up, went back to the three, and found them sleeping.

Jesus (waking Peter): Simon, are you sleeping? Couldn't you wait with Me for just an hour? Stay awake, and pray that you aren't led into a trial of your own. It's true—even when the spirit is willing, the body can betray it.

He went away again, and prayed again the same prayer as before—pleading with God but surrendering to His will.

He came back and found the three asleep; and when He woke them, they didn't know what to say to Him.

After He had gone away and prayed for a third time, He returned to find them slumbering.

Jesus: Again? Still sleeping and getting a good rest? Well, that's enough sleep. The time has come; the Son of Man is betrayed into the hands of sinners. Get up now, and let's go. The one who is going to betray Me is close by.

MARK 14:33–42 THE VOICE

If Jesus, fully human and fully God, perfectly righteous and without sin, needs to journey through life in community with others, isn't it safe to assume the same is true for us? Don't we also need friends with whom we can celebrate the joys of life and then turn to when we feel ashamed about something we did or said or a decision we made that didn't pan out quite the way we expected?

I can't tell you how many times, in different seasons of life, my dear friends have sat me down, looked me in the eye, and said, "We are worried about you."

You see, I am one who prefers to function independently, apart from mere mortals who need basic necessities like food and sleep and heartwarming hugs (Darth Vader, remember). I think I can handle it all—until I can't. I like to think I can do it all—until it all starts to unravel. The real problem is that I will never admit my weakness—pride is my kryptonite. I choose, instead, to live in secrecy and shame until my friends pull me out of the pit and into the light.

I do realize, however, that not everyone has friends who recognize when one of their own is dying a slow emotional or spiritual death. Not everyone has such intimate fellowship that when you all breathe the same air so effortlessly yet one of you takes in a little less oxygen, the others feel the strain.

If you are one of those people who do not have close fellowship, what do you do? Where do you go? Who helps you breathe? What is the first step toward leaving secrecy behind and walking in the light? You muster up all the courage you can find, from your pinky toe to the top of your head, and you find your fellowship, because that is what John the Baptist tells us to do (1 John 1:7).

Over the past two years, my daughter has been shuffled between four soccer teams. Before finding out who else is on her team, I always give her the same speech: "This will be a chance to make new friends. It will be fun." Yet, on the inside I am secretly praying, "Lord, please give her one friend. All she needs is one person she knows. Just one." One friend can make or break a season.

So pause for a moment and think of one person. One friend. Someone in whom you can confide. Maybe it's your husband. Maybe your sister, your friend, a pastor, a neighbor? There is someone. You might not feel like it, but there is. Someone is out there who longs to be your person. You just don't know it yet. Keep praying for God to reveal that someone to you. Don't stop praying until He does.

Now that you know to whom you can turn, let's make a plan. God does not want you living in darkness. He wants you living in the light—with Him! I know it seems intimidating to think you are about to uncover a place of hurt and shame, but trust me, friend, God does not want you walking this road alone. Remember what my son, Campbell, said: "It has to hurt before it heals." So let's commit to heal Mad Libs style:

I will contact   via   by

_____   _____   _____
(person)   (text, phone, e-mail)   (date)

and ask to get together for   by

_____   _____
(coffee, lunch, dinner)   (date)

Congratulations! You just took the first step toward stepping out of shame and walking toward redemption, moving from darkness and into the light!

Let's Get Physical

All this shame-carrying causes more than just emotional and spiritual imprisonment. When we succumb to shame, we internalize fears and guilt that God never meant for us to bear. These emotional burdens express themselves physically. Look at the list below. Do you recognize any of these physical manifestations?

- weight gain (from overeating)
- weight loss (from undereating)
- flushed cheeks
- dizziness
- tunnel vision
- inability to focus
- loud rushing in the ears
- chest constriction
- not being able to make eye contact
- depression
- anger
- suicidal thoughts or actions

Living in the darkness of shame takes a toll on our bodies that we cannot ignore. The apostle John confirms the link between our physical health and our spiritual health: "Dear friend, I pray that you may enjoy good health and that all may go well with you, even as your soul is getting along well" (3 John 1:2). If we are emotionally and spiritually sick, our bodies react with negative consequences. Conversely, if we are emotionally and spiritually healthy, our bodies feel healthy and alive, just as John asserts.

If you notice any of the physical symptoms listed above, I encourage you to talk to your doctor or seek professional help. While I never want to discount the power of prayer, sometimes we also need medical help to combat matters of the physical world.

Passion and Purity

When I was in college, you couldn't walk into a Christian girl's dorm room without the literature trifecta sitting on her nightstand: *Lady in Waiting* by Jackie Kendall and Debby Jones, *Passion and Purity* by Elisabeth Elliot, and *Life on the Edge* by Dr. James Dobson.

Back up to high school and all good Christian girls joined thousands of our sisters in signing True Love Waits pledge cards to vow chastity until marriage—or Christ's return, whichever came first.

The problem is, true love doesn't always wait. According to research:

- 80 percent of unmarried young adults ages eighteen to twenty-nine are having sex.[5]
- 37 percent of women obtaining abortions identify themselves as Protestant, and 28 percent identify themselves as Catholic.[6]
- 50 percent of Americans have cohabitated at one time or another.[7]

I was raised in the generation of preachers, youth pastors, and church propaganda all telling us sex was wrong, wrong, wrong.

Until our wedding nights. Then, not only was sex right, right, right, but we were told to immediately flip the mental switch, have sex whenever it pleased our husbands, and enjoy it every single time. The church told us purity was an all-or-nothing game. One wrong choice and we were deemed "damaged goods." Women with regret and shame were left to carry guilt that was too much for the church to bear. So the church silently stamped a scarlet letter on thousands of young women who then turned inward and have now spent years, if not decades, suffering in silence. I pray we do a better job with our daughters' generation.

Woman at the Well

Jesus is not in the business of shame; He is in the business of redemption. If a woman could cast off her lens of shame and see herself through Jesus' lens of redemption, could she truly live a life of freedom?

Let's ask the Samaritan woman.

It was just an ordinary, yet extraordinary, day—as was every day prior to an encounter with the living and breathing God. A woman showed up at a well to draw water at the hottest time of the day. Why? Because she was consumed with shame. Embarrassment. Humiliation. Regret. She had already had five husbands, and as Jesus pointed out, the man with whom she was currently living was not her husband. Make that six men who had shared her bed, but who's counting? So this woman forced herself to the well at the time of day when she assumed, and hoped, she would be the only person there. Only she wasn't. Jesus was there. Waiting for her. Their meeting was not a coincidence; rather, it was a divine encounter designed to bring glory to the Father.

> *The woman said, "I know that Messiah" (called Christ) "is coming. When he comes, he will explain everything to us."*
> *Then Jesus declared, "I, the one speaking to you—I am he."*
> *Just then his disciples returned and were surprised to find him talking with a woman. But no one asked, "What do you want?" or "Why are you talking with her?"*
>
> JOHN 4:25–27

For a man to talk to a woman he did not know in private was controversial in that time period; for Jesus to talk to a woman of her reputation was downright scandalous. Thankfully, Jesus was more worried about her salvation than His own social status or reputation.

Can you imagine this woman's shock as she and Jesus conversed? Had any man talked to her with such respect? With such genuine kindness and concern? Remember what we said earlier in the chapter? Giving a voice to our shame, stepping out of the darkness and silence and into the light is the beginning of freedom. The Samaritan woman was just beginning to dip her toe into the waters of deliverance.

Scripture continues, "Then, leaving her water jar, the woman went back to the town and said to the people, 'Come, see a man who told me everything I ever did. Could this be the Messiah?' They came out of the town and made their way toward him" (John 4:28–30).

Not only did the Samaritan woman believe in the Messiah, but she also left her belongings and told others about Him. Can you picture her running to the middle of the town and telling every person who would listen, "Come, see a man who told me everything I ever did"? She was openly admitting to the people every sin she had committed. But she didn't care! She had just encountered the Messiah! When you stand face-to-face with the Messiah, all shame and embarrassment and humiliation fade away—you experience freedom! When we experience freedom, we want others to experience the same thing.

John then added:

Many of the Samaritans from that town believed in him because of the woman's testimony, "He told me everything I ever did." So when the Samaritans came to him, they urged him to stay with them, and he stayed two days. And because of his words many more became believers.

They said to the woman, "We no longer believe just because of what you said; now we have heard for ourselves, and we know that this man really is the Savior of the world."

JOHN 4:39–42

The Samaritan woman encountered the Messiah. She engaged in conversation with Him. Then she evangelized. Does this look like a woman bound up in shame, or a redeemed woman running free?

When I was in college I attended a Bible study called "Women at the Well." To this day it is still one of my favorite Bible studies because of its raw, authentic, come-as-you-are message aimed at every young girl yearning for freedom.

I remember it vividly, even though it took place almost twenty years ago (and yes, I am dating myself). We started meeting in the hot, Texas summer. Just a group of soul-searching, Christ-following girls led by one fearless woman—Amy. I didn't even know her last name. Still don't.

We met in a run-down, unassuming building. No workbooks. No organized sign-up list. No worship band. No offering. Just a group of girls meeting together to learn and grow and connect.

Women at the Well—that's what we called ourselves. We were women living on a college campus filled with Living Water, yet many of us were dying of thirst. Even so, somehow we found ourselves drifting toward one another. There we were, each one of us in this tattered building every week. We gathered. We prayed. We listened. We searched. We cried. (Of course we cried; we were college girls filled with hormones and drama.) We participated in twenty-four-hour prayer vigils. We attended the first-ever Passion conference, led by Louie Giglio in Austin. We donated money for worthy causes. (Okay, most girls donated their parents' money, but who's counting?)

Yet, more than just checking off a bunch of do-good items from a list, we underwent heart and soul transformations. Through God's Word, we experienced revival in our little piece of the world. Each day we were filled with more passion for Jesus than the day before, and we realized greater purpose for our lives.

Fast-forward almost twenty years. I long to revisit my Women at the Well encounter. I ache for a place to experience that no-frills, grassroots, approachable community once again. I desperately want a place where women can link arms with other women who look nothing like us and everything like us. I want to find that place where we can talk about God and Jesus, our faith, and the messiness of life. . .all in the same breath. A place where shame is cast aside and women live out their redemption. Does such a place exist? Or is it a mere enigma in my Pollyanna world?

No, I know this unicorn exists. I know because I see the Samaritan woman knocking on doors, telling her neighbors about the Messiah who defeated her shame and redeemed her life. I see Rahab transform from harlot to hero. I see the bleeding woman suffer for twelve years, only to be released from her pain and shame. And the truth is, in Jesus Christ, we all are redeemed. We all are set free. The choice is ours. Will we see ourselves through our lens of shame or through Jesus' lens of redemption?

As Jesus Sees. . .You

What if the Samaritan woman chose not to see herself as Jesus saw her, through His lens of redemption? What if she continued to see herself as she, and the many men with whom she shared a bed, saw her: through a lens of shame. What would her life have looked like? Where would she have gone after she filled her bucket with water? What would have happened to the "many more" who became believers? Take a few moments to jot down the answers to those questions in the space provided.

_____

_____

_____

_____

_____

_____

Thankfully we don't have to imagine the answers to those questions, because the Samaritan woman didn't stay shackled to her shame. She believed Jesus and saw herself through His lens of redemption. What courage, what faith, what trust it must have taken for her to overcome the lies and the mind-set she had been stuck in for so many years.

What about you? What if you choose to continue seeing yourself through your lens of shame? What will your life look like? Jot down a few thoughts here.

_____

_____

_____

_____

_____

_____

Now, what if you choose to cast aside your shame and see yourself through Jesus' lens of redemption? How will that change your view of yourself?

_____

_____

_____

_____

_____

_____

Elizabeth Oates

As Jesus Sees. . .Your Relationships

Shame makes us feel unworthy and unlovable. It makes us want to hide in dark corners, away from the light. Fortunately, for us, our God came into the world to love the unworthy and unlovable, and His light shines brightest in the dark.

Many of us see ourselves through a lens of shame for one reason or another. Yet think of the freedom we would experience if we stopped seeing ourselves through our lens of shame and started seeing ourselves as Jesus sees—through His lens of redemption. How would that affect your relationships?

Ponder this: When we choose to stay stuck in our shame, in our darkness, we lose opportunities. Opportunities to:

- encourage others
- support others
- minister to others
- share the Gospel with others
- grow in our relationship with our Savior
- meet other people's needs
- meet or even exceed our potential
- learn something new
- celebrate and enjoy life
- be thankful

Now circle the things above that you most want to embrace as you move toward a posture of redemption in your life. If you want to add anything, use the space provided below.

_____

_____

_____

_____

_____

As Jesus Sees. . .Your Community

If you could see as Jesus sees, through His lens of redemption, how might this affect your life? Would you stop sneaking out to draw water in the heat of the day like the woman at the well and instead dive in deep with the people in your community? Take some time to journal some changes you would like to make in your life after switching your lens from shame to redemption.

_____

_____

_____

_____

_____

_____

_____

_____

_____

_____

_____

_____

_____

_____

_____

As Jesus Sees. . .Your Relationship with God

What about your relationship with God the Father? If you could see past your shame and see yourself as redeemed, how would your relationship with your Creator look different?

Scripture reads, "My dear children, I write this to you so that you will not sin. But if anybody does sin, we have an advocate with the Father—Jesus Christ, the Righteous One" (1 John 2:1).

The fact is, we have all sinned and we will continue sinning. Yet what a comforting and even empowering thought to know that Jesus stands alongside God the Father as our advocate. When thinking about who an advocate truly is, I came up with three definitions:

1. A person who speaks or writes in support or defense of a person, cause, etc.
2. A person who pleads for or on behalf of another; an intercessor.
3. A person who pleads the cause of another in a court of law.

Have you ever had someone defend you in such an unconditional way throughout your life? Perhaps you have parents who loved you in such a way. Unfortunately, many women have never known such a love. God, however, stands in the gap for all of those who let us down. God shields us when no one else renders aid. God offers redemption when others label us shameful.

Now that you see God the Father standing alongside Jesus as your advocate, how does this help you see yourself as Jesus sees, not through a lens of shame, but through a lens of redemption? Ultimately, how does this change your relationship with God the Father?

Personal Reflection Questions

1. This chapter focused on shame, which is a deeply personal, private emotion for many of us. As you read through the chapter, did you uncover any hidden areas of shame that you were not aware of? If so, explain.

    - How did you feel as you read through this chapter and processed this area (these areas) of shame? Was it difficult? Freeing? Scary?

    _____

    _____

    _____

    _____

2. Elizabeth writes, "Like self-loathing, shame is also a place of darkness, secrecy, and silence." How do you see this playing out in your own life?

    - Do you have plans to change this in the future? If so, how?

    _____

    _____

    _____

    _____

    _____

3. When it comes to shame and redemption, what is your usual approach? Do you allow Jesus into the darkest places in our soul? Or do you withdraw, crawling into the recesses of your mind far away from anyone who can help, and live a life of isolation and deterioration?

_____

_____

_____

_____

_____

_____

4. Elizabeth provides a list of ways in which our shame manifests itself in physical ailments. Have you experienced any of these in your life? Explain.

_____

_____

_____

_____

_____

_____

_____

5. What were you taught in regard to sex and purity when you were growing up?

  • How has that affected you as an adult?

_____

_____

_____

_____

6. In what ways do you identify with the Samaritan woman?

  • What do you learn from her encounter with Jesus?
  • How does this apply to your life today?

_____

_____

_____

_____

7. Elizabeth provides a list of ways in which we lose out on opportunities when we stay stuck in our shame. Did anything on that list resonate with you? If so, what?

  • Did you add anything to the list? If so, what?

_____

_____

_____

Group Reflection Questions

1. When it comes to shame and redemption, what is your usual approach? Do you allow Jesus into the darkest places in your soul? Or do you withdraw, crawling into the recesses of your mind far away from anyone who can help, and live a life of isolation and deterioration?

2. Elizabeth talks about the need to live in community when tackling shame and living in darkness. She also challenged readers to name one person whom they could contact as a first step toward living in the light.

   - Did you take this challenge? Why or why not?
   - If so, how did it go?

3. Elizabeth provides a list of ways in which our shame manifests itself in physical ailments. Have you experienced any of these in your life? Explain.

4. In what ways do you identify with the Samaritan woman?

   - What do you learn from her encounter with Jesus?
   - How does this apply to your life today?

5. Elizabeth provides a list of ways in which we lose out on opportunities when we stay stuck in our shame. Did anything on that list resonate with you? If so, what?

   - Did you add anything to the list? If so, what?

Chapter 4

My Lens of Incompetence, His Lens of Talent

I'm not going to lie, I am probably the last person in the world who should write this chapter (which, in God's eyes, probably makes me the most qualified person to write it). I spent my entire college career floundering from one major to the next because I was told I would never be able to get a job with an English degree. So I stuffed my talents and interests and tried to become someone I was not: a business major.

Now, let's pretend for a moment that I was even slightly interested in numbers, which I was not. I have never been able to balance my checkbook (this was before the days of online banking, so all you millennials can feel free to gloss over that last statement). I don't know the difference between net and gross income, no matter how many times my husband explains it to me. (Is it gross that the government takes that much money, or is it gross that this is how much money I bring home? I can never remember.) No matter how much I studied, all those numbers and statistics sounded like Charlie Brown's teacher (*wah, wah, wah, wah, wah*). I felt lost. I graduated, nonetheless, with a BA in business administration—a degree so vague and useless it doesn't even exist at my alma mater anymore. Well done, good and faithful student.

After graduation I spent time in a job I hated (shocker) and was terrible at (even bigger shocker) because I was completely incompetent. I showed up at the office every day and drew water from a dry well. Simply put: I wasn't using the gifts and talents God gave me.

So, what's a girl to do when she's stuck in a job she hates and is no good at? She prays. She investigates options. Then she looks for doors to open and close.

I eventually quit my job, accepted a totally different career at Dallas

Theological Seminary, and a semester later began attending classes there part-time. It was in seminary that I rediscovered my love for writing and teaching. I remembered that I actually loved learning and school and studying (when it didn't involve economics or finance or accounting). I began to see myself, not through my own lens of incompetence, but through God's lens of talent. That is my hope for you as we work through this chapter together.

Parable of the Talents

My oldest son, Carter, is an avid reader, and when I say avid, I mean you will never see him without a book. Whenever we run errands, he brings a book so thick it reminds me of one I used to sit on in the backseat before the government ruined all our fun and made kids sit in car seats.

In the third grade, Carter earned the honor of reading the most words in his school's history: six million words. I don't know how many books you have to read in order to calculate six million words, because I can't keep up with this kid. When he started reading, I swore I would be one of those conscientious parents who reads everything before her child reads it, and then God laughed and humbled me and said, "Here you go. Here's a kid who can read more in a day than you can read in a year. Have fun with that." I am currently working on my record of zero words for this year, so there's that. But I am raising four little people. We all have our strengths.

My daughter, unlike Carter, is not much of a reader. Clarey would rather create or craft. God has given each of them unique talents. What I love is that neither of them hoards their gifts. Carter reads and indirectly encourages his friends to read. Many of his friends' parents tell me that their child reads more because they want to catch up to Carter's millions of words. We love a little friendly competition in the Oates household. Clarey always makes her friends and family little treasures. Who wants a duct tape pillow or a quilted potholder to brighten her day? This girl, that's who! The point is that they are just beginning to discover and use their unique talents. God calls each of us to discover and then use, not hoard, our talents and resources.

Jesus talks about the importance of using our talents—or abilities—in the parable of the talents. In this parable, a talent is money; however, Jesus makes the argument that all of our resources—talents, spiritual gifts, abilities, money, time, opportunities—belong to God. If you have a few minutes, skip on over to Matthew 25 and read verses 14–30 in your Bible. In the interest of time, let me offer a brief recap:

A landowner entrusts his three servants with three different sums of money, and then he takes a trip. The first servant receives the largest sum of money: five talents (considerably more than a lifetime of earnings).[1] He barters and sells and turns those five talents into ten talents (obviously he was a business major in college). The second servant receives two talents. He takes his two talents to the marketplace, where he turns them into four talents (another whiz kid). The third servant receives one talent, but instead of increasing his wealth, he buries it in the ground (English major, perhaps?).

When the landowner returns from his trip, he is pleased with the first and second servants. To each servant he says, "Well done, good and faithful servant! You have been faithful with a few things; I will put you in charge of many things. Come and share your master's happiness!" (Matthew 25:21).

When he discovers that the third slave has buried the talent, the landowner is furious.

His master replied, "You wicked, lazy servant! So you knew that I harvest where I have not sown and gather where I have not scattered seed? Well then, you should have put my money on deposit with the bankers, so that when I returned I would have received it back with interest.

"So take the bag of gold from him and give it to the one who

has ten bags. For whoever has will be given more, and they will have an abundance. Whoever does not have, even what they have will be taken from them. And throw that worthless servant outside, into the darkness, where there will be weeping and gnashing of teeth."

MATTHEW 25:26–30

What can we learn from the parable of the talents? First, we each have different God-given potential. Sometimes that is a tough pill to swallow. Do you feel jealous because your coworker has been given more responsibility than you? Do you wonder, *When is it my turn?* Or maybe you feel overwhelmed with work and family and other responsibilities and think, *Why is it all resting on my shoulders?*

What I would say to you, friend, is that God knows our potential and our capacity. He knows how many plates we can spin before they will all come crashing down on the floor. Sometimes we like to play it safe and spin fewer plates, but is this really challenging? Do we really want to go through life spinning only one plate? How boring.

Sometimes we try adding too many plates. We say yes more than we say no. Before we know it, we are spinning not only our plates, but also three other plates God never intended for us to pick up. Only God knows exactly the right number of plates we need to give our circus act enough of that wow factor.

We all possess different potential. Sometimes we want more; sometimes we want less. Only God knows how much potential lies within us. Our job is not to figure out how much potential we have; rather, our job is to walk obediently one step at a time, and the potential will blossom along the way.

Second, the parable of the talents teaches us that our gifts, abilities, resources, and opportunities do not belong to us. They belong to God, and they are a gift. My husband, Brandon, and I recently became foster parents, and we realize this opportunity is a gift. Writing this book is a gift. Raising my children is a gift. I realize God easily could have given any of these opportunities to someone else. But for some crazy reason He chose us. If our resources belong to God, why do we sit idle pleading incompetency, literally wasting the very gifts God has bestowed on us? When will we wake up and use those gifts for the kingdom's glory?

The third thing we learn from the parable of the talents is that we have a responsibility to steward our gifts well. If your gift is singing, sign up for your church choir. My gift is tone deafness, so I will do everyone a favor and sing at a dull whisper. If your gift is cooking, bake a meal for the widow who lives next door. Opportunities will not always look for you; sometimes you need to look for opportunities where you can serve others.

Another thing Jesus teaches us is that we will be rewarded if we use our gifts, talents, time, abilities, and resources for the kingdom. Now, don't think Publisher's Clearing House is going to knock on your door just because you mowed your neighbor's lawn for free. God's economy doesn't work that way. What it does mean is that God might entrust you with more responsibility. God might express His joy as He did with the first two servants in the parable. We also know from scripture that we will enjoy this increased responsibility when the earthly messianic kingdom moves to new heavens and a new earth (Revelation 21:1–22:5).[2]

Finally, this parable teaches us that we will be reprimanded for succumbing to fear and squelching—or hoarding—our abilities and resources. God never intended for us to keep our talents to ourselves. What good will they do anyone locked away? God gave us these things to share with others so that ultimately He might receive the glory.

Elizabeth Oates

Unfulfilled Potential

We often tell our son Carter, "We want your best work, not your fastest work." This scrawny little speed demon rushes through everything: eating, homework, bathing. He has great potential if we can just get him to slow down long enough to fulfill it.

What about you? What keeps you from living up to your potential? Many of us fear failure. We are so scared of stepping out on faith and failing that we don't even try. We would rather stay stuck in the land of mediocrity than risk anything extraordinary.

We won't switch jobs even though we are miserable in our current position, because the familiar is less terrifying than the unknown. We refuse to move across the country even though it might provide us with a really valuable opportunity, because we don't like change. All the while we scroll through Instagram watching everyone else live a more interesting life than the one we are pretending to live. Sound familiar?

Think about it: When was the last time you tried something that required more of Jesus—more prayer, more trust, more faith, more uncertainty—and less of you—less planning, less control, less direction, less ego? Have you lived out your faith in a way that actually required risk and trust?

We often worry that we don't have what it takes to succeed. We check out Facebook and Twitter and realize that everyone around us has more followers and friends than we do. We feel incompetent, unqualified, and incapable. So instead of playing the game, we bury our talents in the backyard and call it a day.

There is just one problem with this mentality: this is not what God has called us to do. God has given us each a set of gifts. Instead of wasting time comparing our gifts, overanalyzing our gifts, or wishing we had different gifts, we need to put our gifts into action. Anything else is a sin.

The second reason why we don't live up to our potential is that we fear success. Sounds counterintuitive, but it is reality. We fear what will happen when we actually get what we want. "If my startup company succeeds, I'll have to sacrifice all my free time." Or, "If he proposes, then I'll have to say good-bye to my single life." The things we spend all our time and energy pining for suddenly become the very thing we scorn.

Finally, we don't fulfill our potential because we don't want to pay the price of either failure or success. If we fail, we pay in terms of reputation and humiliation, and maybe we lose some money in the process. If we succeed, we pay with stress, the need to always outdo ourselves, and much more. Either way we pay with our time, which means we also miss spending time on other things, such as family, friends, activities, or hobbies. Everything in life comes with a price tag. That's just the cost of doing life. It's our job to decide how much we are willing to pay.

While I was tucking my daughter, Clarey, into bed one night, she suddenly started sobbing. I'm not talking tears. I'm talking full-on crying, sweating, kicking the covers off, and sitting up in bed boo-hooing.

"What is wrong?" I asked her, confusion on my face, because just two minutes earlier we were giggling and singing a One Direction song.

"I turned in my chicken story today. I wanted to write the best story in my class, but now Boone wrote the best story!" she yelled, eyes shooting darts at me. *Um, when did I become the target of her aggression?*

"What is a chicken story?" I asked calmly, trying to maintain some level of sanity in the conversation. "And why do you think Boone's story is better than yours? Have you read his story?"

"No, but his story is eight pages, double-spaced, one-sided, and mine is only three pages, single-spaced, front and back. So his is longer!" she wailed.

"Okay, but that just means his story is longer," I pointed out, still not understanding the correlation between longer and better. After about twenty minutes of dialogue, it was clear there would be no reasoning with her. In her mind, longer equaled better.

And then my passionate seven-year-old daughter, exhausted from her emotions and distraught from her situation, shouted, "You have no idea what it's like when you have a talent and someone steals it from you!"

There it was. Truth telling.

"Oh, sister, yes I do," I told her as I pulled her into my arms. "I know exactly how you feel." Now she was speaking my language. "Every day I watch people do what I do who are better than me and more successful than me. It stinks when you want to be the best at something but you feel like someone else is better, doesn't it?" I asked empathetically. She nodded her sweaty head against my chest and continued to sob in between breaths. I got it.

I know how it feels to watch high school friends, college friends, and seminary friends live out dreams I had for myself. At times I feel like Forrest Gump, having brushed shoulders with the Christian famous yet never reaching the level of success to which I have aspired. I understand the pain of wanting to have your talent recognized, whether for a chicken story, a book, a business, raising children, or any other endeavor you take on. All of us want our talents acknowledged, our wins celebrated, and our lives recognized. So what happens when they aren't?

As I continued to talk to Clarey, I asked her, "Don't you think there is room in your class for two good chicken stories? There is room in this great big world for all of us to use our talents. If God did not want you to use your talent, He wouldn't have given it to you. Don't waste your gift just because someone else has the same one."

"Does Boone even know about this competition?" She shook her head. "No."

"Does your teacher know? Do your friends know? You have made up this entire competition in your mind. Nobody knows about it but you, and I guarantee you, nobody cares about it but you. Everybody in your class just wants to read a good chicken story, and probably even two good chicken stories."

Sometimes we create competitions in our minds that don't even exist. I told Clarey, and I am telling you, the minute you begin doubting your talents and your gifts, the minute you begin seeing yourself through your lens of incompetence instead of Jesus' lens of talent, capture your thoughts. As Paul instructed, we need to "take captive every thought to make it obedient to Christ" (2 Corinthians 10:5).

The Impact of Social Media

Facebook, Twitter, Instagram, Snapchat, Pinterest, Foursquare, and all the other social media outlets we use are beneficial for connecting people, sharing information, and making the world seem a little smaller. These sites have allowed us to reconnect with old friends and family members, stay in touch with long-distance acquaintances, maintain professional relationships, create new business ventures, promote a vision or a cause, encourage a hurting friend, spread the Gospel, and virtually change the way our world functions.

Even so, researchers are discovering a downside to social media. The Barna Group recently conducted a survey and found that when practicing Christian women compare themselves to their friends through social media outlets, they are:

- eleven times more likely to say their friends "are better than me" in status and privilege;
- ten times more likely to say their friends "are better than me" in creativity;
- three times more likely to say their friends "are better than me" in accomplishing tasks; and
- two times more likely to say their friends "are better than me" in their career or job.[3]

Have you ever mindlessly surfed Facebook, only to shut your laptop, feeling lonely, useless, and discouraged? I know I have. It seems everyone around me has her life figured out. Everyone has a great career. Everyone is popular. Everyone takes vacations. Everyone's kids are all-stars.

The sad thing about social media is that some days it sucks all the joy out of life. After looking at everyone else's posts, I forget two things. First, people show only their highlight reels, not their full footage. They don't post the fight they had with their husband (although some people do air their dirty laundry, but don't even get me started on that soap-box rant); they don't show the time they lost their patience with their toddler; they don't show the credit card bill they can't pay; and they don't show their unkempt lawn that is about to get them kicked out of the homeowners' association. They simply show the pretty, shiny, happy snippets of their lives that they want the world to see, because these are the parts that make them feel good about themselves.

Second, when I waste my time looking at other people's blessings, I forget about my own. I, too, have a great job. Although it doesn't carry much street cred with my kids, the flexibility of freelance writing allows me to attend their school field trips and be home when they get off the bus. I, too, have great friends; we just don't splatter our pictures on social media every time we meet for coffee or dinner. And my children are also all-stars. Just maybe not in the same ways as everyone else's.

The point is that we get so busy playing the comparison game that we don't see the incredible gifts, talents, resources, and blessings God has given us. We see ourselves through a lens of incompetence instead of through Jesus' lens of talent.

So what is the answer? Many people go on media fasts or limit their tech time. Other people limit their followers or try to keep it all in perspective. The answer is different for everyone, and the solution may vary with our changing seasons of life.

I recently read the book *Me Before You* by Jojo Moyes. If you haven't read this fictional tale and you like a good sob story, I encourage you to grab a box of tissues and a few friends with whom you can commiserate, and clear your calendar for a week, because you won't want to put this book down.

In *Me Before You*, the hero of the story, Lou Clark, struggles with feeling incompetent in every area of her life. She is the classic underachiever in her family, even behind her older sister, who brings home an illegitimate child. Until someone—a least likely someone—believes in her. Will Traynor encourages her and makes her believe she is capable of more than she ever thought possible. He opens her eyes to a world she never gave herself permission to believe was possible for herself.

I won't give away the ending, but with only twenty pages left of *Me Before You*, I sobbed like a baby with diaper rash and texted my friends: I AM ALMOST DONE, AND I DON'T KNOW IF I CAN FINISH. IT ISN'T FAIR. NO MATTER WHAT HAPPENS AT THE END OF THE BOOK, EITHER WAY, IT ISN'T FAIR. WHY IS LIFE SO CRUEL? I KNOW LOU AND WILL AREN'T REAL PEOPLE, BUT SOMEWHERE SOMEONE IN THE WORLD IS DEALING WITH THIS VERY ISSUE RIGHT NOW. THEY ARE HURTING AND CRYING, AND IT ISN'T FAIR.

Um, dramatic much? Do you feel sorry for my friends yet? It's a burden to be a receiver of my text messages. My friends deserve gold medals. And wine. (Mostly wine.) The thing is, Lou Clark didn't realize her full potential—the range of her talent—until someone believed in her. We all have a talent waiting to be discovered, and even if no one else sees your talent, Jesus sees.

As Jesus Sees. . .You

Maybe you don't have a Will Traynor who sees your gifts and talents and is cheering you on from the sidelines. But you do have Jesus. He sees you. He knows you. He has been rooting for you since before your life came to fruition. Jesus wants nothing but the best for you, because the best for you means the best for His people and the best for His kingdom.

Isaiah the prophet writes:

> *The Eternal One will never leave you; He will lead you in the way that you should go. When you feel dried up and worthless, God will nourish you and give you strength. And you will grow like a garden lovingly tended; you will be like a spring whose water never runs out. You will discover there are people among your own who can rebuild this broken-down city out of the ancient ruins; You will firm up its ancient foundations. And all around, others will call you "Repairer of Broken Down Walls" and "Rebuilder of Livable Streets."*
>
> ISAIAH 58:11–12 THE VOICE

If you could see yourself as Jesus sees you, through His lens of talent, how would it change you? Would you see yourself as more confident and equipped? Would you see yourself as one whom God can grow "like a garden lovingly tended"? Can you even imagine an almighty God taking the time to gently care for you in this way? He has, He is, and He will.

If you could see as Jesus sees, through His lens of talent, would you feel more capable and competent in pursuing what God has called you to pursue? Would you have the courage to pursue something you have always dreamed of doing? Would you see yourself, as Isaiah describes, as a "Repairer of Broken Down Walls" and a "Rebuilder of Livable Streets"? You have it in you, my friend. You just have to own it.

Take a few moments to answer the following questions in the spaces provided:

What are a few of your God-given talents?

_____

_____

_____

_____

_____

In what areas do you feel most confident?

_____

_____

_____

_____

_____

In what areas have you had the most success? Explain.

_____

_____

_____

_____

_____

As Jesus Sees. . .Your Relationships

Natalie Grant sings a song that I love and I think speaks to the heart of so many women. It's called, "Burn Bright." You should be glad I'm writing about the song and not singing the words (because my singing voice is not joyful noise). In one part of the song, Natalie sings about people who are waiting and ready to blow out our last spark and how we should stay strong and not give anyone permission to dim our light or blow it out completely. The song then goes on about how we were made for more. . .we are to shine brightly for all the world to see.

Have you ever allowed someone to "rain down on your last spark"?

• Explain the situation.

_____

_____

_____

How did it affect your relationship?

_____

_____

_____

If you could see as Jesus sees, through His lens of talent, how could you burn bright?

_____

_____

_____

If you could see as Jesus sees, through His lens of talent, could you embrace your own God-given uniqueness and talents and stop comparing yourself with others? Explain.

_____

_____

_____

If you could see yourself as Jesus sees, through His lens of talent, how would it change your relationships with others?

_____

_____

_____

As Jesus Sees. . .Your Community

Whether we realize it or not, our talent greatly impacts our community and the world around us. When I first started writing this section of the book, I thought about the remarkable women of our generation who are making a global impact through their socially conscious businesses. I love their products, their missions, and their hearts. I wonder how they balance it all: their work, their families, and all the commitments they make. Yet I also admit that sometimes I feel a little left behind. I see them on social media globetrotting to New York and Ethiopia and Guatemala while I am stuck at home trying to choose between fish sticks or pasta for dinner.

Then I thought about the women who—like you and me—live a little more under the radar. God gives us all opportunities to impact our communities, and I don't want us to lose sight of that. I don't want any woman to think that using her talents is an all-or-nothing choice: that we have to either start a worldwide campaign or sit at home and watch another season of *The Bachelor*. So let me tell you about some of these "ordinary" women, and perhaps their stories will resonate with you:

- *Liz, married, mother of two.* Liz recently retired from being a full-time stay-at-home mom and returned to her career as an eighth-grade English teacher. After only two years back at teaching, she won Teacher of the Year for her district. Liz is a typical mom who juggles grading papers, cooking dinner, loving her husband, tending to her children's individual needs, and still trying to maintain friendships and church commitments. She admits maintaining the balancing act is tough, but she always does it with grace and joy.

- *Rachel, associate minister, single woman, and foster mom.* After realizing foster families' great needs when taking in a foster child, Rachel, along with a friend, cofounded Vault Fostering Community to provide tangible resources and support for other foster families. While all of this sounds impressive, most days Rachel just focuses on giving her foster daughter the one thing she needs most—love.

- *Jordan, married, mother of four.* Jordan is a master juggler as she balances life as a stay-at-home-mom and her home-based business/Etsy shop. Wherever Jordan is, you can find her investing in the people around her, whether that's college students, engaged couples, or newly married brides. Jordan is efficient with tasks but even more interested in people—a rare combination in someone as solid and steady as Jordan.

When we compare ourselves to those impacting their communities on a global scale, the task seems daunting. We think, *I'm not competent enough to pull that off.* So we feel tempted to do nothing instead of something.

Pause for a moment and think, *If I stopped seeing myself through my own lens of incompetence and started seeing myself through Jesus' lens of talent, how would it change my community?*

Better yet, *If I stopped seeing myself through my own lens of incompetence and started seeing myself through Jesus' lens of talent, how could I influence and encourage the people around me to pursue their dreams?*

Don't get so caught up in what other people are doing that you miss out on what God has planned for you. "As it is written: 'What no eye has seen, what no ear has heard, and what no human mind has conceived'— the things God has prepared for those who love him—these are the things God has revealed to us by his Spirit" (1 Corinthians 2:9–10).

As Jesus Sees. . .Your Relationship with God

Take a moment to reread Isaiah 58:11–12 from *The Voice*:

> *The Eternal One will never leave you; He will lead you in the way that you should go. When you feel dried up and worthless, God will nourish you and give you strength. And you will grow like a garden lovingly tended; you will be like a spring whose water never runs out. You will discover there are people among your own who can rebuild this broken-down city out of the ancient ruins; You will firm up its ancient foundations. And all around, others will call you "Repairer of Broken Down Walls" and "Rebuilder of Livable Streets."*

Verse 11 tells us that God will "nourish you and give you strength" so that you will "grow like a garden lovingly tended." God wants to nourish your talent, not so you can sit at home and needlepoint, but so that you can go out into the great wide world and impact it for His glory.

If you could see as Jesus sees, through His lens of talent, how would this impact your relationship with God? Would you recognize how God has cultivated the talent you possess? Would you walk through the doors He has opened? Would you accept life's challenges knowing He has lovingly equipped you for each tumultuous step?

Personal Reflection Questions

1. In the parable of the talents, do you see yourself as the first/second servant or as the third servant? Explain.

_____

_____

_____

_____

2. Elizabeth lists five things we learn from the parable of the talents. Which lesson(s) resonate with you and why? (Circle, then explain below.)

   - We each have different God-given potential.
   - Our gifts, abilities, resources, and opportunities do not belong to us; they belong to God, and they are a gift.
   - We have a responsibility to steward our gifts well.
   - We will be rewarded if we use our gifts, talents, time, abilities, and resources for the kingdom.
   - We will be reprimanded for succumbing to fear and squelching—or hoarding—our abilities and resources.

_____

_____

_____

_____

_____

_____

3. Do you feel like you are living up to your potential?

   - If not, what prevents you from doing so? (Fear of failure? Fear of success? Something else?)

   _____

   _____

   _____

   _____

   _____

   _____

4. When was the last time you tried something that required more of Jesus and less of you?

   - Describe the situation.
   - How did it turn out?

   _____

   _____

   _____

   _____

   _____

   _____

   _____

5. What impact has social media had on your view of your talents and capabilities?

- Do you view yourself in a better or worse light after you spend time on social media? Explain.
- Do you feel like you need to make any changes to your social media habits in order to improve your self-esteem? If so, what changes do you need to make?

_____

_____

_____

6. If you could see yourself as Jesus sees you, through His lens of talent, how would it change you?

- Would you see yourself as more confident and equipped?
- If you could see as Jesus sees, through His lens of talent, would you feel more capable and competent in pursuing what God has called you to pursue?
- If so, what is God calling you to pursue?

_____

_____

_____

_____

_____

_____

Group Reflection Questions

1. In the parable of the talents, do you see yourself as the first/second servant or as the third servant? Explain.

2. Elizabeth lists five things we learn from the parable of the talents. Which lesson(s) resonate with you and why?

    - We each have different God-given potential.
    - Our gifts, abilities, resources, and opportunities do not belong to us; they belong to God, and they are a gift.
    - We have a responsibility to steward our gifts well.
    - We will be rewarded if we use our gifts, talents, time, abilities, and resources for the kingdom.
    - We will be reprimanded for succumbing to fear and squelching—or hoarding—our abilities and resources.

3. Do you feel like you are living up to your potential?

    - If not, what prevents you from doing so? (Fear of failure? Fear of success? Something else?)

4. When was the last time you tried something that required more of Jesus and less of you?

    - Describe the situation.
    - How did it turn out?

5. What has the impact of social media had on your view of your talents and capabilities?

    - Do you view yourself in a better or worse light after you spend time on social media?
    - Explain.

6. Do you feel like you need to make any changes to your social media habits in order to improve your self-esteem?

    - If so, what changes do you need to make?

7. If you could see yourself as Jesus sees you, through His lens of talent, how would it change you?

    - Would you see yourself as more confident and equipped?
    - If you could see as Jesus sees, through His lens of talent, would you feel more capable and competent in pursuing what God has called you to pursue?
    - If so, what is God calling you to pursue?

8. If you could see as Jesus sees, through His lens of talent, could you embrace your own God-given uniqueness and talents and stop comparing yourself with others? Explain.

    - If you could see yourself as Jesus sees, through His lens of talent, how would it change your relationships with others?

9. Discuss how you answered the question, "If I could stop seeing myself through my own lens of incompetence and start seeing myself through Jesus' lens of talent, how would it change my community?"

10. Better yet, "If I could stop seeing myself through my own lens of incompetence and start seeing myself through Jesus' lens of talent, how could I influence and encourage the people around me to pursue their dreams?"

Chapter 5

My Lens of Inadequacy, His Lens of Acceptance

One book (Okay, who am I kidding? One *movie*. . .) that has always captivated me is *White Oleander*. In this movie, which was released in 2002, the main character, twelve-year-old Astrid, is shuffled around from foster home to foster home. Throughout the movie, Astrid wrestles with wanting to be accepted not only by her mother, but also by each new foster placement. . .even the foster placements she detests. Looking for acceptance, Astrid becomes a chameleon. She changes her appearance, her habits, and her preferences all in a desperate attempt to please and win the approval of her foster parents. Despite her good-girl nature and can-do attitude, she is continuously tossed out on the curb like yesterday's trash.

At the end of the movie, we see a once innocent, pure, blond Astrid now transformed into a harsh, cynical, Goth version of herself. Astrid finally realizes she cannot spend her life looking for acceptance from others, especially from her mother. She tells her mother, "You look at me, Mother, and you don't like what you see. But this is the price. . .the price of belonging to you." She acknowledges the pain of looking for acceptance from so many people—especially the person you love the most—and never receiving it.

My guess is that many of us feel like Astrid, bouncing through life from place to place, school to school, job to job, and church to church, wondering who we need to be in order for people to accept us. We feel inadequate, incomplete, and inferior. We wonder where in this world is there a place for us.

Social media doesn't help our descent. Can I get an "Amen"? It seems everyone around us is online famous while we are just famously online. Can you relate? Does it feel like no matter how hard you work, no matter how much you try, nothing you bring to the table is ever enough? We all know this is a lie from the enemy, yet from time to time we believe the father of lies because he is really good at his job.

We look around and see other women who seem more successful, wiser, more attractive, wealthier, more patient as mothers, sweeter as wives, and just all around more put together. And we wonder, *What am I even doing here? Each breath I take is an embarrassment to God.*

Do you struggle with this lie too? If so, can you think back to the first time you felt inadequate? Did you fail to live up to your parents' unreasonable expectations? Did you play the part of the quiet wallflower to your homecoming queen best friend? Are you struggling to find the right career while your peers run on the fast track to success? If so, do you see yourself through a lens of inadequacy, always wondering if you will ever be enough? Do you ever ask yourself these questions:

Am I successful enough?

Am I smart enough?

Am I wealthy enough?

Am I popular enough?

Am I nice enough?

Am I helpful enough?

Am I creative enough?

Am I brave enough?

Am I valued enough?

Am I pretty enough?

Am I thin enough?

Am I just enough?

In one word, am I. . .acceptable?

Rest assured, my friend, you are. God says we are enough simply because He is enough for us. "He said to me, 'My grace is sufficient for you, for my power is made perfect in weakness.' Therefore I will boast all the more gladly about my weaknesses, so that Christ's power may rest on me" (2 Corinthians 12:9).

Throughout this chapter we will explore our need to stop looking through our lens of inadequacy and start looking through Jesus' lens of acceptance. Only through our Savior are we ever truly enough.

Woman vs. Woman

Whether we like to admit it or not, there is an underlying competition among women. Social media sites like Facebook, Pinterest, and Houzz.com don't help our situation as we compare our perfectly decorated houses (who needs a pumpkin wrapped in yarn?), our two-year-old's pirate-themed birthday party (which looks like it was thrown by a professional party planner), and the third vacation the Martins' took this summer (while our family hosted a cannonball contest at the neighborhood pool. . .for the third summer in a row).

Women usually fall into one of three categories:
1. Those who compete with others.
2. Those who compete with themselves.
3. Those who don't compete.

The first type of woman wouldn't dare set foot in Target for Valentine's Day. Her throat constricts at the mere thought of her daughter's arch nemesis waltzing into the second grade with a sparklier, more spectacular Valentine's Day card than her own darling daughter, so she creates her own.

"Oh, you're making a homemade construction paper card this year? How cute. Well, I'm crafting a jazzy photograph trifold card with a Tootsie Pop attached and glitter pom-poms on the envelope. Boom!"

The second type of woman thinks about what she bought last year and tries to top it. "Hmm, last year I bought Ninja Turtles Valentine cards from Target. This year I'll buy Ninja Turtles Valentine cards and tape Tootsie Pops to them. Winning."

The third type of woman drives to Target at 11:00 p.m. the night before the party, buys whatever is marked down 75 percent, and calls it a day.

Disclaimer: I do want to give women the benefit of the doubt. Some moms just enjoy the process of making Valentine's Day cards as a creative outlet. Please hear me: this is not a tirade against creativity and art and free expression. What I am advocating for is that we test our motives against Galatians 1:10: "Am I now trying to win the approval of human beings, or of God? Or am I trying to please people? If I were still trying to please people, I would not be a servant of Christ."

Are we competing against our sisters? Are we seeking approval, praise, and commendation from others, or are we serving Jesus in everything we do?

As a determined, passionate woman, I am not asking you to settle for mediocrity. According to several personality inventories, spiritual gifts questionnaires, and love languages tests I have taken over the years, I need accolades, trophies, and lots of verbal praise. My poor husband. Yet I have also learned the hard way, that:

- people are more important than tasks,
- relationships are more valuable than awards, and
- encouraging others is more life-giving than receiving pats on the back.

Bottom line: when we get caught up in the competition chaos, we look at life through our lens of inadequacy. We compete because we want to prove to ourselves—to someone else or to the world—that we are adequate. What if we took a step back and looked at the situation through Jesus' lens of acceptance? My guess is that we would realize there is room enough for all of us.

It's tough in today's world not to compare ourselves to other women. Everywhere we look on social media, people post their achievements for the entire world to see. That's why the apostle Paul offers this piece of wisdom, "Therefore encourage one another and build each other up, just as in fact you are doing" (1 Thessalonians 5:11). Instead of feeling threatened by our friends, we should make a conscious effort to celebrate them.

I admit, my natural bent, my natural gifting, is not words of encouragement. My nickname in college was "Drill Sergeant." (Between Darth Vader and Drill Sergeant, you are probably wondering how I have any friends. Deep down, I really am a nice person, I promise. Way deep down.) I am great at organizing people and assigning tasks. But sometimes amid the function I forget the feelings.

So I try to go out of my way on social media to congratulate people, to offer heartfelt words of praise to those around me. The fact that I see this as a discipline does not make my words less genuine. In fact, I think it makes my effort more authentic, because I am working against my natural tendency. I truly want to offer people love, praise, and adoration instead of zipping from one task to the next—sometimes I just need to take a deep breath to get there.

One thing I have found through this practice is that when we offer praise to our friends—and especially to our frenemies—our heart condition switches from competitor to teammate. Those combative, negative, frustrating feelings dissipate. Offering heartfelt praise to others often changes our own perspective, and we, too, feel special. We stop looking through our lens of inadequacy. We see other people's strengths, but we see our own strengths as well. Suddenly we are no longer in competition with one another; now we complement each other.

Christine Caine, author, speaker, preacher, and founder of Propel Women, posted on Instagram, "Nothing good comes from comparing our unique call from God with someone else's."[1] Let's make a pact to embrace our unique call from God, to stop competing with one another and start celebrating one another. Let's stop looking at ourselves through our lens of inadequacy and start looking at ourselves through Jesus' lens of acceptance. By doing that, we won't need to compare ourselves to our sisters in Christ, for we will rest in the assurance that God has given us every ounce of talent and opportunity we need to accomplish His plan for us. No more. No less.

Unnamed Women

The Gospel of Luke tells us the story of a woman—a woman who doesn't even have a name.

When we got the call for our foster daughter, we only had minutes to decide whether we would welcome her into our home and into our lives. The caseworker told us basic information: Caucasian. Nine weeks old. Healthy, except for diaper rash. If we said yes to the placement, the caseworker would bring her to our house in one hour. One hour! The kids would be getting off the school bus in exactly one hour. I hadn't showered that day (don't judge). We had no clothes, no diapers, no bottles, nothing prepared for an infant. We didn't even know her name. And yet we said yes.

Ever since that day, I have thought a lot about all the nameless women in the Bible: Pharaoh's daughter, Jephthah's daughter, Pilate's wife. Each one unique and brave. Each one living a quiet yet important life. Each one written on the pages of history because of a pivotal decision.

We spend a lot of time deciding on a name for our children. We pore over baby name books, scour the Internet, and take advice from family and friends. Yet, at the end of the day, is the name really that important? Or is it the actual person we should focus on? The character? The life lived? Is a name just a word hiding the soul?

Luke tells us the story about a widow who dropped her measly mite into the temple treasury, only to be judged by those in her community. Scripture reads, "As Jesus looked up, he saw the rich putting their gifts into the temple treasury. He also saw a poor widow put in two very small copper coins. 'Truly I tell you,' he said, 'this poor widow has put in more than all the others. All these people gave their gifts out of their wealth; but she out of her poverty put in all she had to live on'" (Luke 21:1–4).

To fully understand the story, we must first back up to Luke 20. Luke had just warned against teachers of the law who took advantage of widows just like this woman. Luke says men like this love to "have the most important seats in the synagogues and the places of honor at banquets. They devour widows' houses and for a show make lengthy prayers. These men will be punished most severely" (verses 46–47).

I wonder if the widow felt inadequate. Picture the scene: she stands in the treasury, which is an area located within the "court of the women" in the temple complex. The court of the women got its name because, although both men and women were allowed to enter the court of women, women were not allowed to proceed past that point. So right away the widow entered a place where women were made to feel inferior. She walked in alone. No husband. No children. No friends. Yet she entered anyway to worship through her offering.

The court was about two hundred square feet and contained thirteen trumpets, each one narrow at the mouth and wide at the bottom. Now, a person couldn't just drop his or her offering in any trumpet like we drop our money in an offering plate today. Each trumpet was designated for a specific gift:

- Trumpets 1–2: half-shekel temple tribute of the current and of the past year.
- Trumpet 3: Those women who had to bring turtledoves for a burnt and a sin offering dropped their equivalent in money. This saved the labor of women making separate sacrifices and also spared the embarrassment of those who did not want their offering to be publicly known.
- Trumpet 4: Same thing as Trumpet 3, except people deposited the equivalent of their offering for young pigeons.
- Trumpet 5: Contributions for the wood used in the temple.
- Trumpet 6: Incense.
- Trumpet 7: Golden vessels for the ministry.
- Trumpet 8: Money left over from sin offerings.
- Trumpets 9–13: Money left over from trespass offerings, offerings of birds, the offering of the Nazirite, the offering of the cleansed leper, and voluntary offerings. [2]

Elizabeth Oates

Why the history lesson on the thirteen trumpets? To give you a visual of what this moment in time was like for the widow. She could not simply walk into a room, see one cistern, drop in her two coins, and leave. She walked into the court, which was no doubt bustling with men and women who had a lot more money than her, lived in nicer homes, ate better food, wore fancier clothes, and ran in different social circles. Did she freeze, or did she know exactly where to go? She glanced at the thirteen trumpets and had to make a decision. Which trumpet would she choose?

Some scholars believe the priests announced the amount of each person's gift publicly as he or she deposited it. While this is debatable, the fact that it is even a possibility shows the heart condition of those in leadership at the time.

Can you imagine your church deacon announcing your tithe amount as you place your check in the offering plate? Or your church secretary sending out a church-wide e-mail the minute your automatic withdrawal goes through? This is the kind of public scrutiny the Jewish people faced.

But the widow paid no attention to that. She proceeded to drop her two mites into one of the trumpets. *Clink, clink.* Silence.

Imagine the stares. The judgment. Until Jesus reveals the condition of her heart, which strongly contrasts that of the men in power over her. Jesus said to the crowd, "The plain truth is that this widow has given by far the largest offering today. All these others made offerings that they'll never miss; she gave extravagantly what she couldn't afford—she gave her all!" (Luke 21:3–4 MSG). If we look at the ratios of what people gave that day, this widow offered the largest gift. The other worshippers with large budgets gave gifts they would not even have missed. The men saw the widow as weak; Jesus saw her as strong. Society saw her as an outcast; Jesus saw her as valuable. Everyone saw her gift as inadequate, yet she saw it as acceptable.

Friend, do you realize that, like this widow, Jesus is calling you to abandon your so-called weakness and give what you can for the glory of the kingdom? Stop looking to your left and to your right to see what everyone else in the world is offering. Don't play the comparison game. If the widow had done that, she might never have dropped her two mites into the trumpet. *Clink, clink.*

Through the widow, God teaches us that He wants our "yes"— our willingness, our obedience, and our faithfulness. He wants us to trust that when we are lacking, He will supply. When we feel inadequate, He accepts us. "Not that we are sufficient in ourselves to claim anything as coming from us, but our sufficiency is from God" (2 Corinthians 3:5 ESV).

Isn't that where we want to stand, in the place where we rely on nothing but the fullness and supremacy of Christ? Paul says of Jesus, "He said to me, 'My grace is sufficient for you, for my power is made perfect in weakness.' Therefore I will boast all the more gladly about my weaknesses, so that Christ's power may rest on me" (2 Corinthians 12:9).

Easier said than done, right? Especially for those of us independent types. So, how exactly do we embrace God's grace and acceptance? How do we rely on an invisible God in our weakness? Sometimes it all boils down to expectations.

Great Expectations

Sometimes we fail to grasp God's acceptance because we are too busy clinging to our own inadequacy. We create great, high, out-of-reach, unrealistic, pie-in-the-sky expectations for ourselves. Then when we fail to meet those goals—a self-fulfilling prophecy designed by the unattainable level of our expectations—we wallow in our inadequacy. And the cycle continues.

I am not a competitive person—at least not with other people. I never played team sports growing up; rather, I spun and twirled my way through dance and cheerleading. Why? Because I generally don't like competition. Pit me against a friend or an adversary, and the minute I sense someone encroaching upon me, I retreat. I just don't like competition, which is counterintuitive for this Darth Vader, huh? You would think I'd be swinging my light saber left and right, ready to cut off everyone's hand, right? *Wrong.*

Now, competition with myself? That's a different animal. I am the second type of woman we discussed earlier—the type who competes with herself. The bar I set for myself is higher than the Empire State Building. The expectations and goals I create on a daily, weekly, and yearly basis are often so daunting I feel like a failure before I even get started. Can you relate? Do you ever feel like no amount of success is ever enough? Like expectations always exceed the achievements? Every night I go to bed feeling more inadequate than the night before, and every morning I wake up feeling exhausted instead of rested.

Sometimes this cycle of unrealistic expectations leading to feelings of inadequacy occurs in relationships, too. We expect something from someone: a phone call, a conversation, a certain level of friendship. Yet, when that expectation isn't met, our whole world grows dim. We doubt our relationship. We doubt our history. We doubt ourselves. *No wonder they didn't call me back*, we think. *I'm not worthy of their love, their time, their attention.* So we retreat. We pull inward. And the downward spiral ensues.

Counselor, author, and speaker R. Scott Gornto writes in his book *The Stories We Tell Ourselves,* "We all want to know and be known by another human being. It is one of our greatest needs. Our bodies die within days or weeks if we don't have food, water, or sleep—but our souls die without human connection. That's why solitary confinement—whether self-imposed or not—ultimately results in relational ruin."[3]

Do you ever feel this way? Do you long to be known, to be in deep relationships with other people? Yet at the same time do you create expectations for yourself or for others—maybe without even realizing it—only to feel inadequate when those expectations don't live up to reality?

Maybe inadequacy comes from a different place for you. Are you a perfectionist, someone trying desperately to live a perfect life, maintain a perfect image, work the perfect job, raise the perfect family, and at the end of the day, when you lay your perfect head on the your perfect pillow, you know deep in your heart your loud, crazy, messy, life is anything but seamless? Yet you wake up the next day and live it all over again, slaying your soul in the process.

Eighteenth-century writer and philosopher Voltaire once wrote, *"Le mieux est l'ennemi du bien."* (The perfect is the enemy of the good.)[4] When we consume ourselves with attaining the perfect, we miss out on the good. When we chase after the picturesque child in the perfectly pressed smocked outfit, we miss out on the giggly tot discovering the wonder of Play-Doh and ice cream sundaes—oh, the wonder of ice cream sundaes loaded with sprinkles!

When we chase after the perfect marriage of a thousand smiling selfies instead of digging into challenging, difficult, and refining questions, we are left with a shallow marriage that looks really great on Instagram but is hollow in the home.

When we chase after the perfect body at all costs instead of honoring and embracing the gift God has given us, we live a life of constant emotional and mental torment that looks really great on the beach but is never at peace within.

When we view our prayer life, our Bible study time, and our church service as another box to check on our to-do list instead of something to relish, we are left with a lifetime of dutiful service that lacks relational love.

As Jesus Sees. . .You

If you could see as Jesus sees, through His lens of acceptance, how would this affect your view of yourself? Would you finally be able to shrug off unrealistic expectations and perfectionist tendencies that leave you feeling dry, empty, lonely, and inadequate?

I admit, I like a tidy house. But in my closet lies a pile of clothes stacked eyeball high, because whenever I get dressed, I drop my clothing one piece on top of the other. What if we just dumped our inadequacies on the floor until they piled up to eye level? They would no longer cling to us, weigh us down, or follow us around. Can you imagine the freedom?

Paul tells us to "accept one another, then, just as Christ accepted you, in order to bring praise to God" (Romans 15:7). Did you read that? Christ has already accepted you. All you have to do is surrender to Him. You can do it, friend. You can dump your inadequacies in a heap and experience true freedom. All you have to do is stop seeing yourself through a lens of inadequacy and start seeing yourself through Jesus' lens of acceptance.

As Jesus Sees. . .Your Relationships

If you could see as Jesus sees, through His lens of acceptance, how would that change your relationships? Would you be more willing to invite the new neighbor over for coffee? Would you be more able to serve your spouse?

If you could see as Jesus sees, through His lens of acceptance, could you stand next to your sister in Christ and feel confident instead of inadequate? Could you congratulate her on her success instead of swelling up with jealousy and inferiority?

God doesn't want you to feel inadequate; He wants you to feel included. He doesn't want you to feel lonely; He wants you to feel accepted. He wants this for those in your sphere of influence as well. Take a moment to think of someone in your life you could reach out to who might be feeling inadequate, inferior, or incapable. Then pray about ways in which you can wrap your arms around that person and help that person to feel accepted, included, and accomplished. Feel free to use the space below to journal your thoughts.

_____

_____

_____

_____

_____

_____

_____

_____

_____

_____

_____

_____

_____

_____

_____

_____

_____

As Jesus Sees. . .Your Community

I am part of an accountability/prayer group, which we refer to as BAM. It used to stand for Books-A-Million, although now it stands for something a little more PG-13, so we keep our true identity on the down-low. We met at Books-A-Million because we enjoyed torturing ourselves by sitting outside the store on hot, sticky Texas nights. No husbands, no children, and we could stay past closing time. We ignored the massive numbers of crickets and blood-sucking mosquitoes and lived in our own version of heaven filled with rich conversations, deep friendships, gut-busting laughter, and Jesus.

One of my BAM sistahs (not sisters, because we also like to talk in slang like we are teenagers), Kyna, spent eleven years studying God's Word through Bible Study Fellowship, an international Bible study organization that teaches men and women how to study God's Word. She served in leadership positions and felt comfortable and satisfied in her role in BSF. Until one day when she didn't.

"I don't know what God has planned for me; I just know it's not this," Kyna told us one night at BAM. So without a plan or direction, Kyna stepped away from the people and the ministry she had grown to love.

Only two months after her decision, Kyna received a call from Pam, executive director with a local ministry called Christian Women's Job Corp. Pam asked Kyna to join CWJC in leading a twice-weekly Bible study in the local women's jail. At first Kyna felt hesitant.

"Who am I to lead these women?" she confessed at BAM. She had never engaged in prison ministry. She wasn't trained or equipped. Would these women even accept her? Her feelings of inadequacy held her back. But Kyna does nothing without seeking God's direction, so she prayed fervently. Finally, she felt strongly that despite her inadequacies, this was where God wanted her to serve.

After only a few weeks of digging into God's Word with incarcerated women, Kyna came back to BAM and enlightened all of us. "These women are just like us! They are daughters and moms and sisters and friends." Her feelings of inadequacy were replaced with acceptance. "I feel like God has prepared me my whole life for this," Kyna said with confidence.

Once Kyna looked at her God-ordained assignment through Jesus' lens of acceptance, God was able to work through her. And because of her obedience, faith, and willingness to surrender, Kyna continues to bless numerous women every time she walks into the jail. Jesus' acceptance trumps our inadequacies every single time.

Is God calling you to engage in your community but, like Kyna, you feel inadequate? Don't let your limited education, your lack of training, or your little experience stop you from what God is calling you to do.

As Jesus Sees. . .Your Relationship with God

If you could see as Jesus sees, through His lens of acceptance, how would that change your relationship with God? Would you feel more connected to your Creator? Would your faith be stronger?

Paul writes, "So what should we say about all of this? If God is on our side, then tell me: whom should we fear?" (Romans 8:31 THE VOICE). Take a few moments to journal your thoughts on what you fear. What fears do you possess that prevent you from feeling completely accepted by God?

_____

_____

_____

_____

_____

_____

_____

Now think about the part of the verse that reads, "If God is on our side, then tell me: whom should we fear?" There is power in such words. Paul tells us in the same chapter that nothing—no person, no institution, no tragedy, no disease—can overcome our God's love for us. He accepts us and adopts us into His family. As we close this chapter, take some time to write about what it means to be fully accepted by God. How will your life look differently now that you have embraced this truth?

_____

_____

_____

_____

_____

_____

_____

_____

_____

_____

_____

_____

_____

_____

Personal Reflection Questions

1. In what areas of your life do you feel inadequate? Circle the areas
    that apply to you, then feel free to add any additional thoughts in
    the space provided.

    - Career
    - Role as a wife
    - Motherhood
    - Role as a friend
    - Role as a daughter
    - Bible knowledge
    - Health
    - Appearance

    _____

    _____

    _____

    _____

    _____

    _____

    _____

2. Can you think back to the first time you felt inadequate? If so,
    describe it here.

    - How old were you?
    - What grade were you in?
    - With whom did you live?
    - Who were your friends?
    - What was the situation?

- What led to you feeling inadequate?
- Why do you think it has led to a life-long struggle with inadequacy?
- Any other thoughts?

_____

_____

_____

_____

_____

_____

_____

3. Elizabeth listed some questions (Am I pretty enough? Am I brave enough?, etc.) Go back to the beginning of the chapter and reread that list. In the space provided, write out which of those questions applies to you and why.

_____

_____

_____

_____

_____

_____

_____

4. Elizabeth says women usually fall into one of three categories:

- Those who compete with others.
- Those who compete with themselves.
- Those who don't compete.
    - In which category do you see yourself?
    - How does it play out in your life?
    - How does it affect your relationships with others?
    - How does it affect your spiritual life?

_____

_____

_____

_____

_____

_____

_____

_____

5. In this chapter we talked about expectations and how failing to meet our own self-imposed expectations leads to feelings of inadequacy. In appendix B on page 247 you will find a chart titled "The Fallacy of Inadequacy." This chart is designed to help you work through memories of unmet expectations and identify a pattern in which those expectations lead to your lens of inadequacy instead of God's lens of acceptance. Take some time now to work through "The Fallacy of Inadequacy."

6. Regarding the story of the widow and her two mites, Elizabeth says, "Through the widow, God teaches us that He wants our 'yes'—our willingness, our obedience, and our faithfulness." How does this apply to your life today?

- Is there an area in your life where God wants your "yes" but you are allowing your feelings of inadequacy to get in the way? Explain.

_____

_____

_____

_____

_____

_____

_____

_____

_____

_____

_____

_____

_____

_____

Group Reflection Questions

1. In what areas of your life do you feel inadequate? Circle the areas that apply to you.

    - Career
    - Role as a wife
    - Motherhood
    - Role as a friend
    - Role as a daughter
    - Bible knowledge
    - Health
    - Appearance

2. In your Personal Reflection Questions, you described the first time you felt inadequate. If you are comfortable sharing, please tell the group what you wrote down and describe your experience.

3. Out of the questions listed (Am I pretty enough? Am I brave enough?, etc.), which ones did you write down as applying to you and why?

4. Elizabeth says women usually fall into one of three categories:

    - Those who compete with others.
    - Those who compete with themselves.
    - Those who don't compete.
        - In which category do you see yourself?
        - How does it play out in your life?
        - How does it affect your relationships with others?
        - How does it affect your spiritual life?

5. What did you learn about yourself from working through "The Fallacy of Inadequacy" chart?

    - Why do you think it was titled "The Fallacy of Inadequacy"?

6. Regarding the story of the widow and her two mites, Elizabeth says, "Through the widow, God teaches us that He wants our 'yes'—our willingness, our obedience, and our faithfulness." How does this apply to your life today?

- Is there an area in your life where God wants your "yes" but you are allowing your feelings of inadequacy to get in the way? Explain.

Chapter 6

My Lens of Isolation, His Lens of Belonging

Many women today feel isolated. We try covering up our loneliness and emptiness with can-do attitudes, but over time our grit fades. We attend bridal showers and birthday dinners and make chipper small talk until it almost kills us; all the while our souls burn to embers like a thin piece of paper we just lit on fire.

While standing in a room full of people, we feel lonelier than if we were the only person there. So we slowly retreat until our small talk becomes no talk at all. Bridal showers and birthday dinners take up less room on our calendar, until soon the blank space swallows the pen markings. It started slowly, subtly, but we have officially drifted into isolation.

My friend Stephanie knows isolation all too well. As I write this, her daughter, Addison, has spent seventy-five days (and counting) in the PICU (postnatal intensive care unit). After Addison was born, she spent her first 181 days in the NICU (neonatal intensive care unit). She went home for six days, then, due to signs of respiratory distress, Addison was forced to enter the PICU. Now Stephanie spends every day with Addison in the PICU—in isolation.

"I loved the NICU because it was open and I could see all that was going on—new babies being born and dads rushing in to take pictures, nurses chatting with each other about their plans for the night—and I could talk with other moms that would come in to visit their babies. I was able to make friends in the NICU," recalls Stephanie. "I connected with other moms whose babies were in the NICU for a long period of time, as well as made friends with the nurses. I became 'one of the team' because I joined in on jokes, was the mom that the doctors would ask to comfort other moms, and was the veteran.

"The PICU is definitely different," Stephanie told me,

explaining how her situation leads to feelings of isolation. "Addie has her own room as opposed to a bed space in an open room. I sit in my chair, alone, with Addie most of the day. We play, we sing, we watch movies, but it's definitely odd not being able to talk with other parents. We've been in the PICU for over two months now, and I've not met any parents who have children in the unit. In the NICU I made friends with other parents by the second week. This time we're secluded.

"Hospital life can bring you down," Stephanie went on to explain with complete honesty. "Drab walls, dark rooms for low stimulation, being alone most of the day with your child. It's a lot [to take]."

But while Stephanie's circumstances are isolating, she refuses to surrender to the emotions of isolation, depression, and self-pity.

"I try to combat it so it doesn't overtake me. I bring in bright blankets for Addie's bed, bright clothes for her to wear, and the best-smelling baby shampoos and lotions that I can find. Not only that, but I constantly ask Child Life to bring Addie large toys, like swings and exersaucers, or to visit us with therapy dogs."

Every day women, like Stephanie, feel isolated because of their life circumstances. Other women feel isolated due to changing seasons of life, difficult relationship dynamics, or depression. And let's face it: social media—which promises to bring the world together—often disconnects us. We jump on Facebook and see our friends enjoying supper club—without us. We peruse Instagram only to find a photo of our sister's Memorial Day pool party—the one to which we didn't get invited. We scroll through Twitter and read about our coworker's promotion—the one we wanted. We watch the world spinning faster and faster with each news feed, while we feel more excluded and less valuable.

Bleeding Isolation

In the Bible we read about another woman who felt isolated, lonely, abandoned, and ashamed. There is no mention of her name, her family, her occupation, or her status, only her condition: she is "the bleeding woman." Pause now to read her remarkable, transformative story in Mark 5:24–34.

I have always felt drawn to this woman's story, because I have suffered from chronic migraines since I was ten years old. I know what it means to live in physical isolation—to lie in a dark, quiet room for hours, days, or weeks at a time. At one point in my twenties, I endured a constant, pounding, excruciating migraine that lasted twenty-four hours a day, seven days a week, for six months straight. No relief. Not one single second.

Yet not even this pain compares to the bleeding woman's agony. Verse 25 tells us she was "subject to bleeding for twelve years." We don't know her exact condition. Some commentators say it was a hemorrhage, which is uncontrollable bleeding somewhere inside the body. Others say it probably had something to do with her reproductive system. What we need to keep in mind is that it was not just a simple flow of constant bleeding. She was not on her period for twelve years (although, don't get me wrong, that would be worse than starting your period in the middle of a coed sixth-grade gym class). Her plight was an intense, painful, embarrassing, isolating bleeding condition that lasted for twelve long, excruciating years.

The Gospel of Mark says that she sought out "many doctors," and "no one could heal her." She was incurable. I know what that's like. I have seen many general practitioners, neurologists, pain management specialists, acupuncturists, and more over the years. One of my doctors once told me, "You can't cure your migraines; you can only manage them." Do you know what that's like? That's like someone telling you, "You will be in pain for the rest of your life. I can give you a few tools, but it's your job to manage your pain." It feels defeating at best and hopeless at worst. But not for the bleeding woman. She refused to walk quietly to death's door.

Let's consider the sequestered social life this woman lived. According to Jewish law, when a woman had her monthly cycle, she was considered "unclean" for seven days (Leviticus 15:19–31). That means she could not have physical contact with anyone, nor could she enter the temple. The following people and things were also considered unclean:

- Anyone who touched her was unclean until evening.
- Anyone who touched her bed or anything she sat on was unclean until evening.
- Anyone who slept with her was unclean for seven days.
- Anything she lay down on was unclean.
- Anything she sat on was unclean.

Leviticus continues to outline rules for when a woman bled at any time other than her monthly cycle. At these times the following people and things were also considered unclean:

- Anyone who touched her bed or anything she sat on was unclean until evening.
- Anything she lay down on was unclean.
- Anything she sat on was unclean.

In a nutshell, this woman and anyone who touched her were considered unclean twenty-four hours a day, seven days a week, for twelve years. And while these laws might seem harsh, they were put into place because the Jews believed touching such a woman or object defiled God's dwelling place, which was most sacred and pure.

Now that we know the Law, let's ponder what basic things in life this woman missed: family gatherings, family meals, worship in the temple, and births of friends and family members. She couldn't work, because no one would hire her, and she couldn't go to the marketplace, because no one would touch her or exchange goods with her. In general, she had no social life and no community for twelve years. She didn't belong anywhere.

Scripture does not tell us whether the bleeding woman was

married or had children, but we know that doing even simple, mundane tasks, such as preparing dinner for her family, doing the laundry, and making the beds, was prohibited. For twelve years no one shook her hand. No one hugged or kissed her. No one wrapped his or her arms around her and told her, "You matter. We're glad you're here." Can you imagine living without physical human contact for twelve years?

So when she heard that Jesus, the Great Physician, was in town, she went to Him. She had nothing to lose. She couldn't find peace in her home—her family wouldn't touch her. She couldn't find peace in her community—her townspeople wouldn't look at her. She couldn't find peace in her temple—her church wouldn't worship with her. But maybe, just maybe, this man Jesus would accept her and free her from her isolation. For she thought, "If I just touch his clothes, I will be healed" (verse 28).

Sure enough, the woman touched the fringe of Jesus' cloak, and "immediately her bleeding stopped" (verse 29). What numerous doctors and medications could not achieve in twelve years, Jesus accomplished in a single instant.

Then Jesus did what He always does—He exceeded her expectations. He could have healed the bleeding woman and kept walking. That's all she asked for, right? But, no. He always delivers so much more than we ask. He knows we need more than just physical relief—just ask the bleeding woman.

In verse 34 Jesus says to the woman, "Daughter, your faith has healed you. Go in peace and be freed from your suffering." In no other place in the Gospels does Jesus use the word *daughter*. By using this word, He welcomed her back into the family and restored her to her community; He freed her from her isolation and accepted her.

What about you? Do you see yourself as the bleeding woman saw herself, through a lens of isolation? Or are you able to switch your lens and see yourself as Jesus sees you, through a lens of belonging?

Why Do We Isolate Ourselves?

The bleeding woman isolated herself out of medical and legal necessity. In today's society, however, people isolate themselves for many other reasons. As I previously mentioned, seasons of life propel us into isolation. Sometimes stay-at-home moms struggle with identity. They miss their colleagues, the mental challenges of their previous jobs, and being surrounded by people other than *Sesame Street* characters all day.

A working mom also struggles as she learns to balance the demands of career and home, family and friends, church and community. She might try to wear too many hats on her one precious head as she navigates this new chapter in life.

A young girl moving off to college might feel overwhelmed by all the new responsibilities: new town, new roommate, new classes, new professors, new routine, new friends, new activities, new community, new expectations. Too much new and not enough familiar leads many college students into a downward spiral of isolation, depression, eating disorders, anxiety, and other harmful conditions and emotional effects.

Other life changes seem so devastating and so paralyzing that instead of discussing them with someone, we retreat into the recesses of our minds and slowly shut out everyone around us. You may have experienced some of these life changes:
- Relocating to a new city
- Dealing with chronic illness
- Caring for a terminally ill child or spouse
- Caring for an aging parent
- Dealing with a surprise pregnancy
- Experiencing financial hardship
- Becoming an empty-nester
- Losing a close friend or family member
- Losing a job
- Experiencing disappointment of some kind
- Experiencing grief

Often not just a single event, but two or more events occur simultaneously, leaving us feeling as if we have been hit by a tsunami of pain, grief, and despair.

When life changes such as these occur, they trigger past feelings, stress, and other issues that we don't want to face. So, like scared little girls, we run as fast as our feet will carry us into a safe, dark, quiet cave where no one can find us. We isolate ourselves. We hide from people. We hide from our circumstances. We hide from ourselves. We hide from God. The process of isolation begins slowly and then snowballs until our previously happy, outgoing lives are almost unrecognizable.

Let me give you an example of how this could play out in real life:

Mary is a wife, mother of two, and a CPA at one of the most lucrative accounting firms in her town. Her parents always told her, "Mary, study hard. Develop a good work ethic. If you apply yourself, you will succeed." Mary has worked hard, and now she thinks she is next in line for a big promotion. Unfortunately, life takes an unexpected twist. One Friday afternoon she comes home early and texts her husband: I LOST MY JOB TODAY. He immediately calls her. She refuses to answer her phone. He continues calling and texting her. "Please call me. I'm worried about you," his voice mail message says. She cries but cannot bring herself to talk to him. He comes home from work early and says, "Mary, I'm worried about you. Let's talk about this. It's okay if you lost your job. We have plenty of savings. I have a good job that's not going anywhere. You have time to find another job if you want. Or, if you want to stay home with the kids for a while, that's an option too." Mary just stares out the window, refusing to answer him. After a while she gets up and walks out of the room. The conversation is over.

What issues is Mary facing?

- *Fear of the unknown*: Mary is a CPA, and CPAs are notorious for clinging to security, routine, and predictability. Right now,

Mary doesn't know where she will find a new job.

- *Embarrassment*: Mary hears her parents' voices in her ear: "Study hard. Work hard. If you apply yourself, you'll succeed." *Well, I did study hard and work hard, but I didn't succeed*, she tells herself.

- *Need for (financial) safety*: Mary's mind knows they have savings, but without a job lined up, she worries about how long their savings will last.

- *Pride*: How will Mary admit to her friends and parents that she lost her job?

- *Need for respect*: Mary's identity is wrapped up in her job, and she has a deep-seated need for respect from her friends and colleagues.

- *Wanting to prove something to someone*: Mary longs to prove to her parents and herself that she is excellent in her field.

As you can see, Mary's life change of losing her job brought to the surface many reasons why Mary chose to isolate herself. What about you? Which of your issues are rising to the surface? What are your reasons for pulling away from the people you love? What are the emotions, the fears, and the insecurities that cause you to see yourself through a lens of isolation and prevent you from seeing yourself through Jesus' lens of belonging? Consider the following and circle the ones that apply to you:

- Fear of the unknown
- Self-protection
- Fear of getting hurt
- Embarrassment
- Memories from a traumatic event
- Need for safety
- Shame
- Anxiety
- Aversion to risk
- Need for love
- Regret

- Independence
- Pride
- Need for respect
- Insecurity
- Wanting to prove something to someone

What Does Isolation Look Like?

Isolation presents itself in different ways for different people. We all—introverts more than extroverts—need our alone time. Yet there is a difference between "alone time" and isolation. Alone time helps us recharge our batteries, clear our minds, create space for creative thinking, and accomplish certain goals and tasks. Alone time becomes isolation when we take it to extremes:

- When we consciously withdraw emotionally from family and friends, we isolate ourselves.
- When we purposely avoid people in order to escape conversations, issues, conflict, and confrontation—no matter how minor—we isolate ourselves.
- When we stop participating in activities we once enjoyed, we isolate ourselves.

If you find yourself doing the aforementioned or any of the following, you might be living a life of isolation:

- Spending less time doing the things you enjoy (hobbies, crafts, sports, etc.)
- Having difficulty sleeping
- Feeling lonely
- Zoning out in front of the TV, Internet, or social media for excessive periods of time in order to avoid reality
- Undereating
- Overeating, especially in seclusion
- Turning to alcohol or drugs for comfort
- Experiencing depression

Do any of these behaviors look familiar to you? If so, you might be engaging in isolation, which is dangerous to your mental, emotional, spiritual, and physical health. "It's no secret that people who are socially isolated tend to be at greater risk of health issues, from mood disorders like depression to stress-related chronic conditions like heart disease."[1]

Now, I will probably receive some hate e-mail or some nasty tweets for writing this, but I'm writing it anyway. Why? Because I have lived it. Not on the receiving end, but on the running-away-and-hiding-in-my-cave end. The temptation to isolate is not a sin. We all feel overwhelmed with sadness, loneliness, and hurt at some point in our lives. The act of isolation—refusing to live in community and shutting out the very people who love and fight for us—is a sin. From the moment God created Eve for Adam, God created His people to live in community with one another. When we isolate ourselves, whether to protect ourselves or to punish someone else, we rebel against God's design for creation.

What If Isolation Comes from Another Source?

So far we have discussed isolating ourselves. Yet there are times when we feel like we don't belong because of decisions made by other people: the conversations to which we aren't privy, the parties to which we don't get invited, and the groups in which we aren't included. Sometimes Plastics grow up, burn books contain a hint of truth, and we all get our feelings hurt. Feeling excluded leads to loneliness, sadness, rejection, and hopelessness. If this describes you, take a step back and consider these possible reasons why people might not include you in their social circles:

- They have a long history with each other and a deep bond that cannot be broken.
- They assume you have your own circle of friends.
- They assume you are busy and don't want or need to hang out.
- They are just busy people living busy lives and haven't stopped

to consider your feelings, not out of a mean spirit, but out of the sheer pace of life.

If you feel like someone is purposely isolating you, feel free to talk to her about it. But approach her with love and grace and consider the reasons above before entering the conversation.

You might even take a different approach altogether. First, pray. Ask God whom He would like you to include in your life. Chances are, there are other people just like you who feel like they don't belong. They, too, might be thirsting for friendship and deep connection. Ask God to show you who those people are, then pursue them. Ask them to get coffee, go for a walk, or meet for dinner. Building friendships is scary, especially if you are in the throes of isolation, but with God's help, you can tiptoe out of your cave and face your issues.

Another way to defeat isolation is to volunteer. By volunteering you will meet like-minded people who automatically value you because you share the same passion. You will enjoy spending time together, and getting out of the house will help break your isolation rut.

If you do feel isolated by others, realize that your isolation might be a catch-22. People may in fact be excluding you, but are you exacerbating the problem by hiding in your cave of self-protection? The more removed you are from your community, the less people will ask you to participate in life. The less they ask you to participate, the more you isolate yourself. And the vicious cycle continues.

We think that when we isolate ourselves we diminish our risk: risk of getting hurt, risk of loss, and risk of being disappointed. In reality, isolation itself requires great risk. When we isolate ourselves, we risk missing out on life, love, and all that God has planned for us.

Augustine wrote, "God loves each of us as if there were only one of us." Only *you* can accomplish what God has planned for you. Only *you* can be the friend God needs for someone else. If you are willing to approach those you know in love, seek out friendships, or volunteer, you will find there is a whole world of belonging waiting for you.

Another reality is counseling. Isolation leads to depression for many people, and we can't talk about solutions without offering counseling as one. A counselor will be able to offer other solutions and strategies and assess whether isolation is a pattern in your life or if you have full-blown depression. As much as I wish one chapter in one book could solve all your problems, I am not that naive. I am a huge advocate for professional counseling, and if counseling is the tool you need to walk out of your cave, by all means, pursue counseling.

As Jesus Sees. . .You

If you could see as Jesus sees, through His lens of belonging, how would that change the way you view yourself? When we look at scripture, we see that time and again Jesus welcomes those whom no one else takes in. He always asks those whom no one else invites. He always adores those whom no one else loves. So why would He not love us, too?

Scripture tells us, "You are a chosen people, a royal priesthood, a holy nation, God's special possession, that you may declare the praises of him who called you out of darkness into his wonderful light" (1 Peter 2:9). Did you catch that? You are "a chosen people. . .belonging to God." You belong to Him. You are precious and valuable and sacred, and you are His. Do you believe this truth? How does knowing you belong to God influence your overall sense of belonging in the world? Use the space provided to journal your thoughts.

_____

_____

_____

_____

_____

_____

As Jesus Sees. . .Your Relationships

Life is full of joy. Sometimes we just need to sift through the pain to find it. When we isolate ourselves, we can't see beyond the pain. We see nothing but loneliness, despair, and darkness. That is why the enemy wants us to camp out in isolation, hidden in our caves where it is difficult to find hope and happiness. But God wants us to live in community.

The book of Hebrews says, "Let us consider how we may spur one another on toward love and good deeds, not giving up meeting together, as some are in the habit of doing, but encouraging one another—and all the more as you see the Day approaching" (10:24–25). We want to make sure in the midst of our sadness, frustration, anger, or whatever negative feelings we are clinging to that we are not "giving up meeting together." When we want to pull away from life, we can choose to do any of the following:

- Call a friend
- Meet a friend (for coffee, a walk, a jog, etc.)
- Confide in our spouse
- Reach out for help, whether from a pastor or a professional counselor
- Do something to relax (go for a jog, take a painting class, get a pedicure, etc.)

Avoid the temptation to withdraw. Connect with your community. Link arms with your sisters. Live life with your tribe. Run miles with your people. This is your life—do not spend it hiding in your cave.

Think, for a moment, about all the stars in the dark night sky. Billions of them. All alone. Isolated from every other star. They see one another, yet they never connect. Never interact. A few, however, experience the privilege of joining other stars to form constellations. What makes them so special? Were they brave? Were they compassionate? Or were they simply willing? Which star would you rather be: a lonely star who sits up in the great big sky unnoticed, unrecognized, and unnamed for all of eternity? Or a bright, bold constellation that brings joy and wonder to the world?

Like the constellations, we were made to live in relationship with one another. Don't be a lonely star. Be a constellation.

As Jesus Sees. . .Your Community

If you could see as Jesus sees, through His lens of belonging, how would it change your community? Could you reach out to those in need of a friend, to those in need of a place to belong? Amid extreme physical, emotional, and mental isolation, Stephanie has found a place of belonging.

"How do you manage to feel so connected to people when you live most of your life each day within these four walls?" I asked her.

"Facebook has been a wonderful resource for me," Stephanie said. "Since Addison has a tracheotomy, I've been able to join a Facebook group for mothers that have children with trachs. Before she was born, I also joined a group for sacrococcygeal teratomas. Both have been very helpful in meeting other mothers that completely understand what we're going through. Your situation may not be like ours, but one thing is common between women who feel lonely or isolated—everyone needs a friend. Support groups, whether in person or online, can make a world of a difference. You'll be surprised at how many people can relate to your situation if you're open and honest. Find your tribe. Find a group of people that can relate to your situation," Stephanie suggests.

A few years ago, Stephanie started a blog called *The Vintage Modern Wife* as a fun, creative outlet. Little did she know she would become a part of a blogging community that would grow into her lifeline.

"The blogging community has also been incredibly supportive," Stephanie says. "I started a little blog four years ago and never dreamed that I would have the support that it has brought. They have started fundraisers for our family, sent gifts to Addison, texted us, brought us meals, and truly made us feel Jesus' love. Without the support of my fellow bloggers and readers, I honestly don't think I would be as upbeat and positive as I am. I can come to them for the littlest things, such as prayer for healing of a diaper rash, all the way to large things like bringing us meals at the hospital. Their support uplifts me and inspires me to be the best role model to others in situations like ours."

Through her isolation, Stephanie has found a place of belonging and has created a tribe of warriors for Addison. They call themselves Team Pink Ninja.

"#PINKNINJA came about when my tribe of blogger friends wanted to design a T-shirt for our family to sell as a fundraiser. So many ideas were thrown around, but #PINKNINJA stuck after someone mentioned that Addie was always in pink and that she was a fighter like a ninja. As silly as it sounded, it was the truth! Although the concept was simple, it was perfect. Whenever I need my Team Pink Ninja, I use the hashtag #PinkNinjasUnite, and we all come together for Addie."

If you could see as Jesus sees, through His lens of belonging, how would it change your community? Could you muster up the courage to ask a new friend to church? Would you step out of your isolation and join your neighbor's book club? By breaking out of your isolation, you have the power to change your community and the individuals in it.

Before moving on, spend a few moments in prayer. Ask God how He wants you to transform your community through a lens of belonging. Then write down your thoughts in the space provided.

_____

_____

_____

_____

_____

_____

As Jesus Sees. . .Your Relationship with God

If you could see as Jesus sees, through His lens of belonging, how would it change your relationship with God? Would you feel closer to Him? Would you feel like a part of His family? My friend Stephanie claims that her faith is what has helped combat her feelings of loneliness and isolation throughout her eight-month journey.

"I honestly would be in a very bad place without my faith. I've always had faith in the Lord, but I've been a yo-yo Christian. There are times when I'm on such a high for Jesus, and other times where I believe in Him but don't go to Him as I should.

"When we went to our ob-gyn to find out the gender of our baby, we found out at the anatomy scan that our baby was a girl but also that she had a physical anomaly. We were sent to a maternal fetal medicine doctor and were told our daughter would have a sacrococcygeal teratoma [a tumor located at the base of the spine]. I was scared. All I could think to do was pray. I prayed that God would do great things within Addie. I prayed for Addie's life to glorify Him. That prayer started it all. It brought a fire to my faith again—a fire that had been smoldering and now has been reignited.

"Now that we've been in the hospital for eight months, I have seen firsthand that I have no control over things. Addie has been through six surgeries in her life. We have been told that she's 'a ticking time bomb' and that she could die. Still, surgery after surgery, Addie has pulled through with flying colors. She has defied the odds and continues to be incredibly strong. She is such a special little girl that I know the Lord is working within her. He is using Addison for His works. I am able to see it so plainly, and it strengthens me more and more each day."

I, for one, want to be like Stephanie. I want to revel in a faith that is on fire for God. I want a faith that burns so brightly that its light will illuminate the way for others. I want to say with the psalmist: "You, Lord, keep my lamp burning; my God turns my darkness into light" (Psalm 18:28).

If you could see as Jesus sees, not through your own lens of isolation, but through His lens of belonging, could you have a faith like Stephanie's? Could your faith burn brightly in the darkness? Journal your thoughts here.

Personal Reflection Questions

1. What was your reaction to Stephanie's story?

   - If you struggle with feeling isolated, how did Stephanie's story make you feel about your own isolation?
   - What do you think about the ways in which Stephanie deals with her isolation?
   - How would you respond if you were in Stephanie's situation?

   _____

   _____

   _____

   _____

   _____

   _____

2. In what ways do you relate to the bleeding woman (Mark 5:24–34)?

   _____

   _____

   _____

   _____

   _____

   _____

3. Elizabeth provided a list of life changes that lead to isolation. Do any of these apply to you? If so, which ones?

   • Have you experienced any life changes that led to isolation that were not on the list? Explain.

   _____

   _____

   _____

   _____

   _____

   _____

   _____

   _____

4. Elizabeth describes what isolation looks like for some people. Do you tend to isolate yourself? If so, what does isolation look like for you?

   _____

   _____

   _____

   _____

   _____

   _____

   _____

5. Do you agree with Elizabeth that purposely isolating ourselves is a sin? Why or why not?

_____

_____

_____

_____

_____

_____

_____

6. If you could see as Jesus sees, through His lens of belonging, how would it change you?

_____

_____

_____

_____

_____

_____

_____

_____

Group Reflection Questions

1. What was your reaction to Stephanie's story?

    - If you struggle with feeling isolated, how did Stephanie's story make you feel about your own isolation?
    - What do you think about the ways in which Stephanie deals with her isolation?
    - How would you respond if you were in Stephanie's situation?

2. In what ways do you relate to the bleeding woman (Mark 5:24–34)?

3. Elizabeth provided a list of life changes that lead to isolation. Do any of these apply to you? If so, which ones? Have you experienced any life changes that led to isolation that were not on the list? Explain.

4. Elizabeth describes what isolation looks like for some people. Do you tend to isolate yourself? Explain.

    - If so, what does isolation look like for you?

5. Do you agree with Elizabeth that purposely isolating ourselves is a sin? Why or why not?

6. In the Gospel of Matthew, we read, "And when the Pharisees saw [Jesus having dinner with tax collectors and sinners], they said to his disciples, 'Why does your teacher eat with tax collectors and sinners?' On hearing this, Jesus said, 'It is not the healthy who need a doctor, but the sick'" (Matthew 9:11–12).

- How does this passage relate to the themes of isolation and belonging?
- How does this passage relate to your own life?

7. If you could see as Jesus sees, through His lens of belonging, how would it change you?

Chapter 7

My Lens of Discontentment, His Lens of Generosity

Late one night when I should have been sleeping but was instead wasting time on Facebook, one of my foster mom friends posted a comment.

"I got eight kids!" she wrote in response to an online quiz, the kind of ten-question test you take to escape chores, kids, book writing, sleep, and reality of all types.

Suddenly several of my foster mom friends weighed in, so I took the quiz too—although I admit I felt a little apprehensive. I thought the quiz, in only ten short questions, would reveal all of my insecurities and failures as a human being and as a mom.

As I said earlier, I currently have four children—three biological kids plus one foster—and I thought the great quiz master behind the green curtain would tell me I had caused irrevocable damage to them all and should have quit after one or two. Why? Because I like security, predictability, and organization. If I had it my way, I would put a For Sale sign in the front yard and go live in the Container Store. I would wear a whistle around my neck and carry a bullhorn at all times. A girl can dream, can't she? Yet I do realize I am raising little people and not an army of minions, so I pray for grace, compassion, patience, and many other attributes sweet, adorable mamas possess.

Despite my need for order, I wanted three kids my entire life. Growing up, I had only one sibling, a brother. He was four years older than me, and we might as well have lived on different planets. We had different interests, different friends, and we attended different schools. Although we are fiercely loyal to each other today, growing up we spent little time together and rarely connected.

I wanted something more for my children, something deeper, a closer bond nurtured in childhood that would grow into adulthood. So

I planned it out, much like I plan most of my life. Three kids close in age. Best friends. They would giggle together, play games, and defend one another against playground atrocities. There would be chaos and activity and frenzy wherever we went, but it would all stem from love and laughter. Well, I was right about the chaos, activity, and frenzy part. Like most siblings, they play well and fight well, and along my parenting journey I have learned that both the laughter and the squabbles come with the territory of toting around a small army, especially now that we have added a fourth child to the mix.

So there I sat, staring at my computer, about to take a test revealing my magic kid number:

12

You seem like you're mentally capable of handling twelve kids. You just need a little bit of financial and emotional support so that they'll have a great upbringing (and maybe a decent education) and you can maintain a bit of sanity for simple daily tasks. A little pro tip would be to not take them to the grocery store all at the same time. But overall, it shouldn't be too hard for you—you've done harder things in life, and plus, you excel at getting things done, even when they seem impossible.

Best of luck with your little army!

I do like order and predictability, but I also like chaos, fun, noise, and people, so I guess twelve littles running around makes sense after all. Whew! Crisis averted.

The interesting thing to me was not the number revealed, but the logic behind that number. "You just need a little bit of financial and emotional support so that they'll have a great upbringing (and maybe a decent education)." How did an innocuous Facebook quiz know about my deep-seated financial anxieties? How did it know that for months I had been wrestling with this very issue—so many kids, so little money?

This was supposed to be fun, Facebook! Not a therapy session!

This past year I put my part-time job teaching yoga and Pilates on hold to focus on writing, which sounds artistic and fanciful and every writer's dream, except when the brutality of reality sinks in.

When I said good-bye to my yoga mat (albeit temporarily), I also said good-bye to my part-time income. As Murphy's Law always plays out, our family took several financial hits after we made this significant decision. Did I make the wrong decision? Was God testing our faith? I don't know.

What I do know is that leaving a part-time job I loved to pursue a dream and then dealing with some unexpected events was not what I signed up for. "Um, God, remember the deal we made? I follow your call, and you bless me. That's how this thing works." Only it didn't. Our situation brought to the surface a host of anxieties, fears, and insecurities that I thought I had long ago dealt with and buried forever. Yet here they were again, rising to the surface.

Through much conversation, prayer, and spiritual wrestling, I asked myself many tough questions—questions you will explore throughout this chapter—including these:

- Am I discontent?
- Is God enough?
- From where are my insecurities stemming?
- How has God provided for me in the past?
- What would it take for me to feel secure, content, and happy?
- Am I willing to be content with less than what I think I deserve?
- Will I trust God to provide for me in the future?

When I took a step back and looked at the big picture, I knew I needed to ask myself one overarching question. As we begin this chapter, I want you to ask yourself this same question: *Am I looking at my life through a lens of discontentment, or am I looking at my life through Jesus' lens of generosity?*

By the way, my husband took the test too. It told him he should have fifteen kids. Yikes!

Am I Discontent?

We live in America: land of the free, home of the brave. Our culture shouts:

- "Pull yourself up by the bootstraps!"
- "If you work hard, you will succeed."
- "Go ahead and buy it; you deserve it."

Sorry, America, but your American Dream mentality flies straight into the face of scripture. Jesus is all about love and grace, not sweat equity and long hours at the office. Yes, a strong work ethic and honesty are virtues we want to embrace, but those qualities will not usher us into the gates of heaven. Unfortunately, many people in our culture still struggle with discontentment as they bow down to the holy altar of success, prosperity, and greed all in the name of security, responsibility, and leadership.

So let's challenge ourselves, shall we? Let's test our lives, not against our neighbor's standard of living or what our parents taught us or even what our pastor preaches from the pulpit. Instead, let's examine our lives according to what scripture teaches. Maybe then we can answer the question, "Am I looking at my life through a lens of discontentment, or am I looking at my life through Jesus' lens of generosity?"

In Matthew 20:1–16 we read a parable about a wealthy landowner. This parable teaches us about the ugliness of discontentment that drives many of us—myself included—into a pit of bitterness and dissatisfaction. In this parable, Jesus tells about a wealthy landowner and a group of day laborers. Picture the scene: A landowner goes out early in the morning and sees a large group of men waiting to be hired for the day. He chooses only some of them to work in his vineyard and agrees to pay them a denarius, the usual daily wage. The men get to work.

Can you imagine how the rest of the men felt? Discouraged. Frustrated. Disheartened.

The wealthy landowner returns at 9:00 in the morning and then again at noon to pick two more crops of men, promising to pay them "whatever is right" (verse 4). The remaining men wonder why they were not chosen. Will they ever be? They wait, feeling daunted and anxious. Morning turns into afternoon.

At 3:00 p.m. the landowner shows up again. Despair turns into joy as a third group is chosen. The wealthy landowner must have had a lot of work to do on his property, because scripture tells us, "About five in the afternoon he went out and found still others standing around. He asked them, 'Why have you been standing here all day long doing nothing?' 'Because no one has hired us,' they answered. He said to them, 'You also go and work in my vineyard'" (verses 6–7).

At the end of the day, the landowner pays all the day laborers one denarius. Well, you can imagine that doesn't sit well with everyone, especially people like me who possess a great need for equality and justice for all.

"So when those came who were hired first, they expected to receive more. But each one of them also received a denarius. When they received it, they began to grumble against the landowner. 'These who were hired last worked only one hour,' they said, 'and you have made them equal to us who have borne the burden of the work and the heat of the day.'

"But he answered one of them, 'I am not being unfair to you, friend. Didn't you agree to work for a denarius? Take your pay and go. I want to give the one who was hired last the same as I gave you. Don't I have the right to do what I want with my own money? Or are you envious because I am generous?'

"So the last will be first, and the first will be last."

MATTHEW 20: 10–16

I admit, until recently I wrestled with this parable. Why? Because I read the parable through the lens of the discontented early morning worker.

My husband, Brandon, calls me "the grinder." I was the girl in high school who took copious notes, studied four days before the big test,

Elizabeth Oates

and barely squeaked by with a B in geometry. I was the grinder.

He, on the other hand, never cracked a booked, studied thirty minutes the night before an exam, made a 100, and graduated fourth in his senior class. But I'm not bitter. I am totally at peace with it. Can't you tell? (Wink, wink.)

The early morning workers responded with envious hearts. Despite receiving exactly what the landowner promised and what they agreed to, they wanted more. Why? Because the early morning workers didn't think equal wages were justified. They failed to look through the grateful lens of those hired late in the afternoon.

Can you imagine the angst of the men hired late in the day? Their fear? Their worry? If you have ever been unemployed with a mortgage to pay and children to feed, then you know the dread these men must have felt. How could they go home and tell their wives and children they had earned nothing that day? They could not. So they stayed. And they waited. And they waited some more. They never gave up hope. And eventually the landowner returned for them.

The first lesson we learn from this parable is that discontentment blinds us from seeing the plight of those around us. Despite the landowner's generosity, the early morning workers could not see how their own peers were in need. This happens to us, too. We spend an exorbitant amount of money on clothes that will be out of style next season, forgetting that some women don't even own a single suit they need for their first job interview. We pine away for a bigger house with a game room and a pool, forgetting that children just eight miles away live in deplorable conditions with no running water or electricity. We work evenings and weekends, chasing that big promotion, forgetting that many people lack necessary skills to land a decent job. We are so hyper-focused on getting what we want that we fail to see the desperate needs of those sitting right next to us.

This parable also teaches us that when we look through a lens of discontentment instead of Jesus' lens of generosity, we fail to see God's generosity toward others. The early morning workers should have celebrated the landowner's generosity toward the other workers, not sulked over it. When one of us succeeds, we all succeed. When one person becomes a productive member of society, we all reap the benefits. Why do we waste time and energy despising someone else's success when we should be cheering for one another?

A popular quote flooding Instagram and Pinterest reads, "Her success is not your failure." What wise words for today's woman. We look all around us on social media and even in our own communities and we see woman succeeding, which is great! We want women to succeed, to flourish, to blossom in the gifts and talents God has given them. But when you see others succeed, do you feel your own stock diminish? Or can you genuinely celebrate your different spheres of influence? Do you feel greedy in terms of how much you want, how soon, and at what cost?

The third thing we learn from the parable of the wealthy landowner is that discontentment prevents us from seeing how God has blessed us. The landowner paid the early morning workers one denarius—a fair wage, a common wage, and the exact wage he promised them. If the workers had looked through the landowner's lens, they never would have succumbed to discontentment. They would have realized the landowner was not slighting *them*; rather, he was blessing the *other* workers. But instead of looking at the situation through the landowner's perspective, they allowed their selfishness and insatiable craving to overtake them.

Has this happened to you? Have you watched someone in your own life receive something you wanted, something you thought you deserved, and allowed your greed to overrun your life? Maybe a coworker received that sought-after promotion. Maybe a friend moved into your dream home. Maybe you have played the part of the bridesmaid, but never the bride. Do you feel like an early morning worker in life, always playing by the rules only to feel overlooked at the end of the day? Or are you looking at life through Jesus' lens of generosity, realizing the many blessings He bestows on you and me and everyone else who doesn't deserve them? However difficult, anytime we are left feeling slighted, upstaged, or empty-handed, we must succumb to a spirit of generosity, knowing that all we have is an open-handed gift from our Savior.

Is God Enough?

When we give in to discontentment, we fervently say with the very breath God gave us, "God, you're not doing enough. You're not providing enough. You are not enough." So we take matters into our own hands. We work harder. We accumulate more. We trust less. We shine more, while He shines less. We rise to the top, while pushing our Savior to the bottom.

If we are not careful, discontentment can snowball into greed. Is the word *greed* unsettling to you? Maybe you have never thought you struggled with greed. It really is an ugly word. Who wants to admit to being greedy? Only misers like Uncle Scrooge and Cinderella's wicked stepmother are greedy. Yet, in reality, greed rests within the deep recesses of each of our hearts.

Jesus even warns us about greed. "Watch out! Be on your guard against all kinds of greed; life does not consist in an abundance of possessions" (Luke 12:15).

We need to identify the areas of greed and discontentment in our own lives so we can eradicate them for our own mental, emotional, and spiritual health. The day laborers were concerned about money, but maybe you are mentally, emotionally, and spiritually preoccupied with something else. Take a look at the list below. Which of the following things causes you to feel discontent? Circle the ones that apply to you. Feel free to add anything that is not listed.

- Opportunities for yourself
- Opportunities for your children
- Popularity
- Security/stability
- Status

- Success
- Wealth/financial security

When it comes to greed, it is not only our own personal well-being that is at stake. Proverbs says, "When the greedy want more, *they stir up trouble*; but when a person trusts in the Eternal, he's sure to prosper" (28:25 THE VOICE, emphasis added). Everyone around us suffers when we submit to greed. We become self-centered and nearsighted. We withhold compassion. We deny love. We refuse to help others. We stir up trouble. We damage our Christian witness.

If, however, we trust in God to provide for us, if we say God is enough for us, then, as Proverbs tells us, we will prosper. How can we not choose the more peaceful path where God drives and we enjoy the ride, knowing His journey leads to peace while ours leads to controversy and conflict?

From Where Is My Discontent Stemming?

Now that we know in what area of life we struggle with discontentment, we need to figure out from where it stems.

My oldest son recently complained about not being able to see the whiteboard at school. I, being mother of the year, ignored him. I have kids to raise, dinner to cook, and deadlines to meet, people. I can't be bothered with trivial things like mere eyesight. My oldest, however, is quite persistent (shocker). He continued complaining, so finally, halfway through the second semester of the school year, I asked his teacher if she noticed anything. She said she had already sent him to the nurse's office twice and he had passed both vision screens. Um, I didn't even know he had been tested. Again, mother of the year. No applause necessary.

I decided to stop perusing Pinterest and take him to the pediatrician. Diagnosis: Carter is nearsighted. He sees things close up but not far away. He needed glasses. Okay, you may applaud now.

Our adventure into the land of the nearsighted reminded me of the story of the prodigal son. In this story from Luke 15, a man has two sons. One son is obedient, hardworking, and loyal—much like the early morning workers of the parable of the wealthy landowner. The second son is the complete opposite: lazy, selfish, and rebellious.

The second son, widely known as the prodigal son, asks his father, "Father, give me my share of the estate" (verse 12). The son might as well have said, "Dad, I wish you were dead."

Despite the lack of respect, his father obliges. Scripture tells us that his father divides his property between the two brothers. The older son stays home and continues working for his father like any duty-bound son would. The younger brother leaves, and scripture says he "squandered his wealth in wild living" (verse13). Then when he hits an emotional, spiritual, and financial rock bottom, he returns home to the forgiving, open arms of his father.

What we see in the younger son is that he, too, is nearsighted. He sees only what is right in front of him: the parties he wants to attend, the drinks he wants to consume, the ladies he wants to entertain. He doesn't see how his immediate actions will affect him—or his family— long term. He is selfish and immature and can't see beyond his greed.

What about you? Is your discontentment a result of nearsightedness? Are you seeing only what is right in front of you instead of looking at the big picture?

Let's consider another possibility. Maybe your discontentment stems from wanting to fit into the world instead of wanting to fit into heaven. The apostle John writes, "Everything in the world—the lust of the flesh, the lust of the eyes, and the pride of life—comes not from the Father but from the world" (1 John 2:16). When we want the world, instead of eternity, we become discontent.

Here are some other sources of discontent to consider:
- Arrogance
- Dissatisfaction
- Fear
- Insecurity
- Lack of trust in God to provide
- Impatience

- Selfishness
- Status

Do any of these ring true in your life? Do you see any of these attributes play out in your everyday existence? If so, know that Jesus wants more for you. He wants you to lay down your discontent in exchange for His fullness. As the apostle Paul writes, "I pray that you, being rooted and established in love, may have power, together with all the Lord's holy people, to grasp how wide and long and high and deep is the love of Christ, and to know this love that surpasses knowledge—that you may be filled to the measure of all the fullness of God" (Ephesians 3:17–19).

How Has God Provided for Me in the Past?

When discontentment wells up in our hearts, it eclipses all the goodness and beauty that used to reside there. We live in darkness, suffering from temporary memory loss and forgetting the many ways in which God has met our needs—and wants—in the past.

I mentioned that our family endured a difficult season. What made this season even worse was my reaction. I allowed my insecurities and fears to overshadow the truths I knew. I saw my life through my own lens of discontent: how *I* wanted my life to look instead of the way *God* wanted my life to look.

Even in my darkest hour, scripture reminded me, "If we are unfaithful, He remains faithful, for He is not able to deny Himself" (2 Timothy 2:13 THE VOICE). When I found it difficult to rely on God's promises for me, I clung to this one promise—that He would remain faithful until the end. If you are in a place of despair, I encourage you to hold fast to this promise as well. God will remain faithful until the end. He will never change. He will never leave. He is your one constant.

Eventually, through conversations with Brandon, prayer, and poring over scripture, I began seeing our situation through Jesus' lens of generosity. Brandon reminded me over and over again of how God had provided for us in the past.

God might not have answered my prayers the way I wanted, and He might not be answering your prayers the way you want, but God is sovereign. The stinging truth is that God owes us no explanations for His decisions, and He looks to no one for approval.

Jeremiah tells us, "Ah, Sovereign LORD, you have made the heavens and the earth by your great power and outstretched arm. Nothing is too hard for you" (32:17). Intellectually, I knew God had provided for us and would continue to do so. He has the power to do this—nothing is too difficult for Him. Emotionally, I had to accept that His provision just might not look the way I wanted it to. That was a tough pill to swallow.

So I began working through all the ways in which God has provided for me, both financially and otherwise. I want you to do the same. My guess is that I am not the only person who struggles with remembering how God has provided for me over the years.

So please take a few moments to turn to the "God's Provisions" chart in appendix C on page 250. Spend some time filling out this chart, which has three purposes:

1. To help you remember God's faithfulness.
2. To give you something concrete to refer to when you doubt God's goodness and faithfulness in your life.
3. To show you all the blessings you already have so that when discontentment creeps into your heart, you can squelch it with the abundant blessings God has already given you.

Remember, this is not for a grade. There are no right or wrong answers. Ready. Set. Go!

What Would It Take for Me to Feel Secure, Content, and Happy?

In the midst of our difficult situation, Brandon remained cool, calm, and collected, as always, which only made my anxiety increase, because I felt like I had to carry the burden for us both. Then he asked this question: "What would it take for you to feel secure?" His question caused me to pause, because I don't think there was a large enough dollar amount. And that was the problem.

Think about it. What would it take for you to feel secure? Content? Happy? Is there any amount of money, success, popularity, or status that could fill up your life and make you feel whole, complete, and satisfied?

Am I Willing to Be Content with Less Than What I Think I Deserve?

When answering Brandon's question, I had to first ask myself, "Am I willing to be content with less than what I think I deserve?" It's tough not to succumb to jealousy, envy, and greed when we are inundated through social media with our friends' vacation photos, dream homes, new cars, job promotions, and all the other exciting things people want to celebrate. We are left feeling as if we are living a less-than-stellar life. Just because we are surrounded by people living these lifestyles doesn't mean this is God's plan for us, too. This is the harsh reality some of us must accept.

What is your grim reality? Maybe God is asking you to find contentment in your current job instead of chasing that illusive promotion. Maybe God has something different planned for you other than a traditional pregnancy. Maybe God wants you to move to another city, away from your friends and family. Maybe God is asking you to stay home with your children when you want to work, or He's asking you to work when you want to stay home.

What we need to remember is that what we consider to be a

less-than-ideal situation might be what God considers the ideal situation.

When we do ask God for something, James reminds us to check our motivation. "When you ask, you do not receive, because you ask with wrong motives, that you may spend what you get on your pleasures" (James 4:3). Maybe we do not receive because God knows the greed behind the request.

Another question to consider is, "What price will my family pay?" Proverbs tells us, "The greedy bring ruin to their households, but the one who hates bribes will live" (15:27). When we succumb to greed, whether by running up credit card debt, working late hours at the office, or trying to maintain the perfect image, our spouse and the little people in our homes pay a dear price. Is it better to punish our loved ones for our insatiable appetites or to surrender to a holy God who loves us just as we are?

On the other hand, maybe we ask with all the right motivations and intentions yet still do not receive. Then what? Where do we turn? How do we reconcile our faith? In those trying times, we cling to truths found in God's Word: "Many are the plans in a person's heart, but it is the LORD's purpose that prevails" (Proverbs 19:21).

Will I Trust God to Provide for Me in the Future?

Ultimately, discontent stems from a lack of trust in God. We don't trust God to provide for our financial needs, so we pinch pennies. We don't trust God to orchestrate our professional careers, so we work twelve-hour days, six days a week. We don't trust God to fulfill us emotionally, so we numb ourselves physically by logging extra miles on the treadmill despite a nagging injury.

Jesus said in His Sermon on the Mount, "Seek first [your heavenly Father's] kingdom and his righteousness, and all these things [that you need] will be given to you as well" (Matthew 6:33). If we first seek what God wants for our lives, all of these other things will fall into place.

The Message version of this and the preceding verses says eloquently:

"If God gives such attention to the appearance of wildflowers—most of which are never even seen—don't you think he'll attend to you, take pride in you, do his best for you? What I'm trying to do here is to get you to relax, to not be so preoccupied with *getting*, so you can respond to God's *giving*. People who don't know God and the way he works fuss over these things, but you know both God and how he works. Steep your life in God-reality, God-initiative, God-provisions. Don't worry about missing out. You'll find all your everyday human concerns will be met" (Matthew 6:30–33 MSG).

Relax. God will attend to you. Like a newborn baby, you are His pride and joy. Let Him take care of you.

As Jesus Sees. . .You

If you could see as Jesus sees, through His lens of generosity, how would this affect the way you see your life? Would you see the abundance God has bestowed on you, or would you still long for more? Would you move past discontentment and embrace fulfillment?

Would you give more than you receive? Would you trust more than you worry? Would you pray more than you talk? Take a few moments to journal how you think your life could change if you could start seeing yourself, not through your lens of discontentment, but through Jesus' lens of generosity.

_____

_____

_____

_____

_____

_____

Elizabeth Oates

As Jesus Sees. . .Your Relationships

Our oldest son and daughter were recently baptized, and if that's not enough to make a Mama weep, they were dunked on Mother's Day (insert tissues and sobbing and sentimental hugs, surprising for even this Darth Vader). I remember each child's baby book had a place for me to choose a Bible verse for them, but I never did. How was I supposed to choose a Bible verse when we hadn't even gotten to know each other yet? This time around, I was prepared. Brandon and I talked about their personalities and gifts, and we chose a verse fitting for each child.

For Carter we chose Philippians 4:13, "I can do all this through him who gives me strength." This kid has already fought hard and overcome a lot in his nine short years of life. He is wicked smart (unlike his mother, the Grinder). There is nothing he can't accomplish in this world, and we truly believe he can do all things in the name of Jesus.

For Clarey, our seven-year-old, we chose 1 Corinthians 16:14 (ESV), "Let all that you do be done in love." Clarey is a natural giver. She is compassionate and caring and selfless. She loves all people and all people love her. We wanted to encourage her to continue loving others in Jesus' name.

Some people, like Clarey, are natural givers. She makes cards for all twenty-two students in her class, not because it is Valentine's Day, but because it is Tuesday. Other people, unlike Clarey, are takers. They monopolize conversations, borrow but never return, and always ask, "What's in it for me?"

If you could see as Jesus sees, through His lens of generosity, how would it affect your relationship with others? How would it affect you if you are a taker? Asking yourself this question might be uncomfortable, even difficult. Yet all of us need to step outside of ourselves and ask God how we can minister to others in His name.

Take some time now to pray and ask God how you can act generously toward those in your life. Feel free to jot down what God tells you.

_____

_____

_____

_____

_____

_____

_____

_____

_____

As Jesus Sees. . .Your Community

One of my children's favorite animated movies is *Robots*, the story of a boy robot inventor named Rodney Copperbottom who saves his community from the evil management, Phineas T. Ratchet. In the movie, the boy's hero, Bigweld, repeats his motto—"See a need, fill a need"—which leads to creating successful inventions.

How many of us see needs all around us yet never fill them? We see children lacking in basic reading skills, but we are too busy to start an after-school reading club. We see pregnant teen moms desperate for someone to walk alongside them, but we are too scared to get involved.

If you could see as Jesus sees, through His lens of generosity, how would it affect your community? Would you forget your own discontentment and give more of your time, money, and emotional support?

Take some time to dream big here. What are the needs in your community? Do any of those needs match up with your passions? Spend some time in prayer, asking God to open your eyes to see through His lens of generosity.

As Jesus Sees. . .Your Relationship with God

Paul writes, "Keep your lives free from the love of money and be content with what you have, because God has said, 'Never will I leave you; never will I forsake you'" (Hebrews 13:5).

Have you ever stopped to think about how generous God is with His presence? He never leaves us. He is with us every single day, watching every blink, every exhale, every tear. He wants us to be content, because if we are always in His presence, then we really don't need anything else, do we?

So, if you believe Paul's words, and if you could see as Jesus sees, through His lens of generosity, how would that affect your relationship with God? Journal your thoughts in the space provided.

_____

_____

_____

_____

_____

_____

_____

_____

_____

_____

Personal Reflection Questions

1. In the parable of the wealthy landowner, with which workers do
    you identify most—the early morning workers or the 5:00 p.m.
    workers? Explain your answer.

    _____

    _____

    _____

    _____

    _____

2. On page 154 Elizabeth offers some things that cause women to
    feel discontent.

    - Do you identify with any of these areas? If so, which ones?
    - Are there any areas you added to the list? If so, what?
    - How do these areas of discontent affect your life on a daily
      basis?

    _____

    _____

    _____

    _____

    _____

    _____

3. Elizabeth provides a list of areas from which our greed might stem (see p. 156). Did any of these sources strike a chord with you? If so, which one(s)? Explain.

_____

_____

_____

_____

_____

_____

_____

_____

4. What did you learn from working through the "God's Provisions" chart?

_____

_____

_____

_____

_____

_____

_____

_____

_____

5. Now that you know in which area you struggle with greed, and from where that greed stems, try answering the following questions:

- What would it take for me to feel secure?
- What would it take for me to feel content?
- What would it take for me to feel happy?

_____

_____

_____

_____

_____

_____

6. In this chapter Elizabeth explains how she had to ask herself this question: "Am I willing to be content with less than I think I deserve?" Spend some time asking yourself that question. Then write a letter to God explaining your answer.

_____

_____

_____

_____

_____

_____

_____

7. According to Proverbs 15:27, greed can have a negative effect on our families and relationships. Have you seen this play out in your own life? If so, explain.

_____

_____

_____

_____

_____

_____

_____

_____

8. Ultimately, we want to avoid discontentment by trusting God to provide for us. Practically speaking, what does this look like in your life?

_____

_____

_____

_____

_____

_____

_____

_____

Group Reflection Questions

1. In the parable of the wealthy landowner, with which workers do you identify most—the early morning workers or the 5:00 p.m. workers? Explain your answer.

2. On page 154 Elizabeth offers some things that cause women to feel discontent.

   - Do you identify with any of these areas? If so, which ones?
   - Did you add any areas to the list? If so, what?
   - How do these areas of discontent affect your life on a daily basis?

3. Elizabeth provides a list of areas from which our greed might stem (see p. 156). Did any of these sources strike a chord with you? If so, which one(s)? Explain.

4. What did you learn from working through the "God's Provisions" chart?

5. According to Proverbs 15:27, greed can have a negative effect on our families and relationships. Have you seen this play out in your own life? If so, explain.

6. Ultimately, we want to avoid discontentment by trusting God to provide for us. Practically speaking, what does this look like in your life?

7. How does our culture breed and even reward greed?

   - How can we fight against this in our families?
   - If you have children, how can you teach your children to not succumb to greed?

Chapter 8

My Lens of Burden, His Lens of Blessing

When I think of the word *burden*, I often think of the elderly woman sitting all alone, day in and day out, wondering if and when her family will ever come visit her. Her television is broken, the kitchen sink leaks, she can't drive, and she has nothing more than a few boxes of Jell-O and cereal to last her the week. All her friends have either passed away or live in a retirement home, so she reaches out to no one for fear she will burden everyone.

Have you ever felt like a burden? Maybe your parents divorced and then spent more time arguing over who should pay for your braces and college than they spent actually pouring into your heart. Maybe your mentor at work makes you feel more like a task than a student worthy of her time and attention. Maybe you want to serve at your church, but they don't seem to have a place for you.

Rest assured, my friend, there is always room for you in God's kingdom. We are never a burden to Jesus. God created us, He chose us, and He adopted us. Scripture tells us, "For he chose us in him before the creation of the world to be holy and blameless in his sight. In love he predestined us for adoption to sonship through Jesus Christ, in accordance with his pleasure and will" (Ephesians 1:4–5).

If you have spent the majority of your life seeing yourself as a burden, get ready to switch your lens and see yourself as Jesus sees—through His lens of blessing.

Jesus Loves the Little Children

In the Gospel of Matthew, we see Jesus walking around Judea, talking and teaching while "great crowds" follow Him. Picture Bono walking around the middle of Times Square chatting with the locals. People following Jesus, relentlessly pursuing Him and challenging Him. Some are drawn to His compassion and love. Some trying to understand His new ideology and theology. Others subversively trying to prove Him wrong.

In the midst of Jesus' walking and talking, some people interrupt Him. "One day some parents brought their children to Jesus so he could lay his hands on them and pray for them. But the disciples scolded the parents for bothering him" (Matthew 19:13 NLT).

I love this passage because it is a pivotal moment in the lives of these children. They are standing in a crowd of people. Their parents usher them forward, wanting them to have front row seats to the rock star, but the bouncers turn them away. Why? Because these children are a nuisance and an inconvenience. Children should be seen and not heard. Don't these parents realize this is the Jesus show? How dare they interrupt important kingdom work! Yet, as we will see, at the Jesus show, we all are important to the kingdom.

The crowd holds their breath, waiting to see what will happen next. Jesus' reaction will shape the children's self-image for the rest of their lives. Will they view themselves as a burden or a blessing?

"Jesus said, 'Let the children come to me. Don't stop them! For the Kingdom of Heaven belongs to those who are like these children.' And he placed his hands on their heads and blessed them before he left" (Matthew 19:14–15 NLT)

Jesus takes time out for these children, as He takes time out for you every moment of every day. Do you take time out for Him?

Does this story conjure up painful memories for you? Maybe you, like these little children, stood at someone's side, waiting, longing, hoping to be noticed. Maybe you performed, wanting to gain affection. Maybe you achieved, trying to earn accolades. Maybe you gave, hoping to make friends. Maybe you told jokes, clowning to win laughs. When none of that worked, maybe you rebelled, thinking negative attention was better than no attention. Yet, at the end of the day, you still felt like more of a burden than a blessing to your parents, to your teachers, to your friends, to yourself, to your God.

If we learn anything from Jesus and the little children, it is that we need to stop listening to naysayers like the disciples and start listening to Jesus. The disciples say, "You're not enough." Jesus says, "You are enough." The disciples say, "Go away." Jesus says, "Come to me." The disciples say, "You're in the way." Jesus says, "I am the Way."

Sometimes we think the kingdom belongs to everyone else and we are stuck on the outside looking in. Jesus reminds us in Matthew 19:14 that the kingdom "belongs to those who are like these children"—those who approach Jesus with love and humility and trust and no agenda other than to listen and learn and live life for the kingdom's sake.

Yes, the kingdom belongs to you just as it belongs to these little children, just as it belongs to Moses, Sarah, Abraham, Ruth, Esther, David, Paul, Peter, and all the great men and women of faith who lived before us.

Even so, this truth is difficult and painful to accept if we learned at an early age that we were a burden. Did your parents play favorites when you were growing up—and you were the odd girl out? If so, know that the kingdom belongs to you just as it does to your sibling. Is your boss grooming someone for the big promotion and you are clearly not next in line? If so, know that the kingdom belongs to you just as it does to the person in the corner office. Do you always feel like you stand on the outer edge of the inner circle of friends? If so, know that the kingdom belongs to you just as it does to everyone in every circle and sphere of influence.

God cannot change your past, but He wants to walk with you in your future. Will you stop looking through your lens of burden and see as Jesus sees, through His lens of blessing? Will you believe Him when He says you are loved, beautiful, redeemed, talented, and accepted? Will you believe Him when He says you belong? If you are all of these things, how can you be anything less than a blessing? If you need to move beyond your past and into a glorious future, rely on this truth: "He heals the brokenhearted and binds up their wounds" (Psalm 147:3).

Elizabeth Oates

Burden Bearers

Maybe you feel like a burden, not because of something in your past, but because of your present. Maybe you pursued a friendship with someone only to find that person doesn't have time for you. Maybe you invited a new neighbor over for dinner only to find that she was more interested in the food than the friendship. Maybe you make plans with a friend who consistently cancels at the last minute. Many of us see ourselves as a burden instead of a blessing for several reasons.

First of all, we carry around heavy baggage. I recently took a trip to New York with my BAM sistahs to usher in our fortieth birthdays. I won't reveal who turned forty and who did not, but I will say that if the waiter carded the under-forty crowd, I would have had my ID ready. Every. Single. Time.

As we loaded up our luggage in the back of the car and prepared to drive to the airport, we realized one thing: I am not a light packer. Out of five women, I brought the largest, heaviest suitcase. I pack for every emergency known to man and apparently am the only one in my group of friends who doesn't own a suitcase with wheels. I didn't care though. I was going to New York! With no husband asking me to make dinner and no children asking me to drive them to soccer practice. I had my outfits planned and my massive suitcase packed. I was NYC-bound!

Ironically, I didn't wear half of what I took. My cute shoes were uncomfortable and my skirts were impractical. So I ended up mixing and matching, adding a jacket here and there, and wearing the same three things repeatedly. I probably could have packed everything I needed in a single backpack and survived the week.

What I realized on that trip is that most of us tote around unnecessary baggage in life. We refuse to relinquish things we don't need: hurtful words, painful breakups, job losses, regrets, and disappointments. We stuff them into our emotional and mental suitcases and drag them around with us, adding more and more baggage each year.

Then, one day, our suitcase is so heavy and our spirit so leaden, we sit immobilized.

The second reason we see ourselves as a burden instead of a blessing is because we refuse to break ties with toxic people. Whether a dysfunctional family member, an alcoholic spouse, an emotionally abusive boyfriend, a selfish friend, or an unhealthy church member, people who once seemed like valuable and vital parts of our lives now cause tension and frustration. They bring us mental anguish, always making us second-guess the boundaries we set and the choices we make. Toxic people also cause emotional harm by manipulating our feelings. The stress they cause in our lives leads to physical illnesses such as ulcers, heart disease, high blood pressure, headaches, weight gain, weight loss, and many other ailments. Toxic people sell us a lie that we are the albatross preventing them from succeeding in life—and we buy the lie every time.

Finally, we feel like a burden because we listen to the enemy telling us we are unlovable, ugly, shameful, incompetent, inadequate, isolated, and greedy. He whispers these lies into our hearts and minds and wreaks havoc on our souls. In the beginning we ignore him, but over time his voice gets louder and louder until we can't tune him out. Eventually we tie a millstone of self-loathing around our neck and wade into the water of despair, surrendering to a slow, emotional drowning.

My friend Beth saw herself as a burden for all three of these reasons. She hauled around emotional baggage, which she didn't realize until later. It was almost as if she were carrying around a backpack and Father Time piled bricks in it so slowly that she never noticed, until one day her backpack was so heavy she couldn't take one more step.

"My story starts like a lot of other women's," recalls Beth, "not feeling like myself all the time, waves of sadness and not sure why. Was this a new kind of PMS? What was going on? I didn't want to get up in the mornings, skipping a meal or two didn't matter, and I cried a lot. My eyes were like a spigot without a shut-off valve. As the depression deepened, eventually I stopped taking care of myself and would go for weeks without taking a shower or brushing my teeth. What was the use? I didn't see the purpose of it anymore.

"For that matter, the 'fall' felt like slow motion, but in actuality it was a day-by-day progression and acceleration of feelings of worthlessness, hopelessness, and despair. Eventually I hit rock bottom without realizing what was happening, before things had a chance to get better. But in the middle of it all, I didn't care. About anything."

Beth's depression spiraled out of control to the point where she even contemplated suicide. She could no longer care for her two children, nor could she function at her job. She felt like a burden to her children and her husband.

"At the time [my husband and I] worked together, and I was not capable of pulling my weight in the office like I usually did. I was not capable of responding as intimately as I had before my depression. Depression causes a constant bombardment in every aspect of life. It prevented me from being myself, and I was continuously letting my husband down, which I internalized as 'being a burden.' Physically, emotionally, and with work, I felt like I was letting him down. Our physical, emotional, and spiritual intimacy was being chipped away daily, and as the balance shifted from a positive state to a negative one, the burden became heavier and more difficult to bear. Then one day I woke up and realized I had nothing to give my husband. Depression takes everything you have just to take care of yourself. It is about this point when the positive is completely replaced by the negative in life and suicide starts to sound like a great idea."

Fortunately, Beth never drifted so far into depression that she chose that route. Instead, God sent her a neighbor to pull her out of her darkness and help usher her into the light.

"I was sitting in the yard pulling weeds when Anne, my across-the-street neighbor came out to check her mail," Beth remembers. "Anne walked across the street with her mail and started a light and easy conversation about weeds and bills. Before I knew it, she was sitting down with me, pulling weeds. We didn't even say that much; we were like toddlers in parallel play, happy to sit quietly together, each wrapped up in our own thoughts."

As the days and weeks passed, Beth shared her struggle with Anne, who also wrestled with depression. "One of these mornings, Anne stood up and asked me to go somewhere with her," Beth said. "She was taking me to a doctor. 'Don't worry about the bill,' she said. She and her husband were paying for it."

Beth spent eighteen months of intense therapy with a psychiatrist. Although her road to recovery was long, her spirit was strong, until one day she came home to a letter from her husband. "He had left and was divorcing me. He could not handle the emotional roller coaster ride of my depression any longer."

While Beth was wrecked, she had come far enough in her treatment not to let this blow destroy her. With support from her sister, mother, and Anne, she forged ahead and rebuilt her life.

"I still struggle with feelings of being a burden to people," Beth confesses. "Especially those closest to me. I probably have a tendency to share too much with some people and not enough with others. Sometimes it is easier to tell a total stranger sitting next to you on a plane your true feelings than to let yourself be totally vulnerable with someone you love. Heck, you will never see the person on that plane again! There is so much more riding on the relationship with people you love."

The Martha Affect

Would it help you to know that even Jesus was made to feel like a burden? One of my favorite Bible stories is the account of Mary and Martha, two sisters who were polar opposites.

As Jesus and his disciples were on their way, he came to a village where a woman named Martha opened her home to him. She had a sister called Mary, who sat at the Lord's feet listening to what he said. But Martha was distracted by all the preparations that had to be made. She came to him and asked, "Lord, don't you care that my sister has left me to do the work by myself? Tell her to help me!"

"Martha, Martha," the Lord answered, "you are worried and upset about many things, but few things are needed—or indeed only one. Mary has chosen what is better, and it will not be taken away from her."

LUKE 10:38–42

Usually, the object lesson taught is that presence is greater than presents. Jesus wants our time, not our thyme. The King would rather us sit at His feet, not wait on Him hand and foot.

Those lessons are great when we look at the story through the lens of "How does this affect *me*?" Yet if we look at the story and ask ourselves, "How does this affect Jesus?" we realize how much Martha made Jesus feel like a burden. So much hustle and bustle. So much work to be done—food to cook, tables to set, dishes to wash, linens to fold, centerpieces to create. . .and so on.

Jesus was there, with humble Mary sitting at His feet listening attentively. She gave Him her time and attention. Meanwhile, He quietly watched Martha zipping around the room like an angry queen bee buzzing around her hive.

Do you think Jesus felt welcomed? Do you think He felt comfortable? Do you think He felt well-received or cherished or valued by Martha? My guess is no. My guess is that Jesus felt like a burden to Martha. My guess is that He felt like He heaped another thing on her already lengthy to-do list.

My guess is that we also make Jesus feel like a burden in our own lives. We make Jesus feel like a burden every time we think about spending time in the Word yet quickly trade Bible time for another episode of *House Hunters.* We make Jesus feel like a burden when we begrudgingly sign up to serve in the church nursery and then complain the entire time we serve apple juice to two-year-olds. Jesus doesn't want our service or obligations or excuses. He wants our hearts.

Stop and Smell the Roses

I admit that a lot of Martha resides deep within my soul. I am an action-oriented taskmaster. I like lists and plans and results. So I have to consciously focus on making people—not projects—a priority. But I wasn't always this self-aware.

My freshman year in college I was overwhelmed with the amount of responsibilities suddenly placed on my shaky shoulders. I took fifteen hours of classes, worked thirty hours per week, was involved in too many extracurricular activities, and had just pledged a sorority. Plus I had a social life to maintain. This was college, people! I wasn't just there for an education. Oh wait, yes I was. So, in order to keep my world in balance, I made a sign and hung it on my desk. It read:

PRIORITIES
1. Quiet Time
2. Homework
3. Work
4. Working Out

One afternoon I sat at my desk, diligently working on priority number two, when my friend from across the hall walked in and plopped down on my bed. Kelly, oblivious to the sign I had clearly posted, started mindlessly chattering about the sky, or her nails, or her earthquakes test, or something of equal insignificance. I don't know, because it wasn't on my list of priorities.

I tried to ignore her, but that was virtually impossible. She was from Mississippi, the size of a pixie, had a southern drawl that is too adorable for words, introduced me to all things south of the Mason-Dixon Line (such as grits and cracklins) and was as persistent as crickets chirping on a hot summer night.

Finally, when I realized she was not going to leave, I turned to face her. "Kelly, do you see this sign?" I asked, using my pencil to point to PRIORITIES.

"Yes," she said, giggling, already used to my drill sergeant ways and obviously not taking them seriously.

"Quiet time. Homework. Work. Working out. Those are my priorities. Right now I am trying to do my homework. So, unless you see your name on this list, which you don't, get out." (On a side note, Kelly and I are still the best of friends, and I have truly reformed my bossy ways.)

"Okaaaaay," Kelly said with her very best southern drawl as she stood up very slowly (girls from Mississippi move slower than Yankees, I have learned) and started to leave my room. "Elizabeth, you need to take some time to stop and smell the roses," she said as she sauntered out the door, completely unphased by my Martha ways.

Do you think I made Kelly feel like a burden or a blessing? I all but picked her up with my bare hands and threw her out the door. Clearly I erred on the side of burden. Sometimes we are so shortsighted, so tunnel-visioned in what we need to accomplish, that we make others feel like a burden.

Sometimes we respond to our family and friends out of our own selfishness, forgetting that the attitude is more important than the outcome. How we make them feel along the way is more important than what we do for them.

How many times have I begrudgingly run carpool, cooked dinner, packed lunches, folded laundry, and made snacks, all with a less than stellar attitude? We think doing things is enough, when in reality our kids want us to *want* to do things for them. They don't want us to slap together a turkey sandwich while complaining under our breath. They don't want us to drop them off at their friends' house if we are going to make them feel guilty about the inconvenience. This kind of attitude communicates one thing to their exposed hearts: "You are a burden, not a blessing."

Our friends want us to *want* to check on them when they are having a bad day. They don't want us to feel obligated to call them. What kind of friendship is that? Our husbands *want* us to want to encourage and support them in their careers. The token "How was your day?" will not suffice. We must want to celebrate their victories and console their losses. If we merely deposit the paycheck twice a month and never inquire about the details, what does that say about our loyalty and connection?

One friend recently reminded me of this concept. A friend whose name, ironically, is Rose. "Sometimes I feel like my husband feels obligated to stay with me even if he's not happy," Rose confided in me. "Men aren't very good at communicating how they feel (we all know this) so sometimes my imagination gets the best of me. I feel like maybe he doesn't really love me, but he feels like he has to stay with me."

Rose was expressing honest emotions about feeling like a burden—feelings that a lot of women experience after saying "I do," adding a mortgage and a car payment, tossing in a kid or two, and basically signing our lives away from now until death do us part. Sometimes, if our husbands are the sole breadwinners, we wind up feeling like an obligation instead of their one true love.

"Sometimes I feel like I don't deserve him. Not that he is some outstandingly amazing, perfect man, but I just over worry that maybe I need to do more to make him love me more," Rose said, weighed down by feeling like a burden instead of a blessing.

Burden Prevents Progress

We all want progress in life. We want successes, victories, and achievements. Beth wanted healing in her struggle with depression. Rose wants reassurance and a deeper emotional connection in her marriage. We want to look back on life and know that our time here on earth meant something. It mattered. *We* mattered. But we can't move forward in life if we are laden with burdens.

When the little children approached Jesus, His entourage tried to protect Him. The NIV tells us that Jesus said, "Do not hinder them." Stop getting in their way. Stop preventing them from achieving their goal. Stop putting up roadblocks between them and me.

What about you? Do you feel hindered in life? Do you feel like someone or something is preventing you from achieving your goal or reaching your full potential?

If Jesus calls you to something, no roadblock is too strong. You might experience obstacles on your journey and things that delay your progress. You might even encounter people who make you feel like a burden. But if God calls you to do something, He will make it possible. The minute the cross was lifted up, the roadblocks were torn down.

So how can we unpack our baggage? How can we break the chains from toxic people? How can we stop believing the enemy's lies? How can we overcome our roadblocks? How can we stop seeing ourselves through our lens of burden and start seeing ourselves through Jesus' lens of blessing?

First, as scripture tells us, you must "cast all your anxiety on him because he cares for you" (1 Peter 5:7). Each of us must tell Jesus why we feel like a burden. So pour out your heart. Journal, pray, weep, yell—whatever it takes to cleanse your soul. Why? Because He cares for you. He loves you. He wants you to heal from your past and move into a hope-filled future.

Next, we must accept His truth. "God is so rich in mercy, and he loved us so much, that even though we were dead because of our sins, he gave us life when he raised Christ from the dead. (It is only by God's grace that you have been saved!)" (Ephesians 2:4–5 NLT).

God's truth tells us the following:
- He is merciful.
- He loves us.
- He gave us life when we were dead.
- We are saved because of God's grace.

Those four truths negate anyone who tries to tell us we are a burden. Anyone who argues with God's truth is not for Him but against Him. God's truth insists that we are a blessing. If we listen to the contrary, then we are burdening God.

As Jesus Sees. . .You

Still not convinced? In chapter 2 we read Psalm 139, but let's take a moment to revisit it.

You created my inmost being; you knit me together in my mother's womb. I praise you because I am fearfully and wonderfully made; your works are wonderful, I know that full well. My frame was not hidden from you when I was made in the secret place, when I was woven together in the depths of the earth. Your eyes saw my unformed body; all the days ordained for me were written in your book before one of them came to be.

PSALM 139:13–16

When I was pregnant with my second child, we decided not to find out the gender. We already had a son, and Brandon thought this time around the surprise would be fun. I thought he was crazy. I decided, however, to dabble in submission and agree to his wish. It was not a good idea. I was cranky and antsy and did not enjoy not knowing who this tiny person was inside of me.

The summer before our baby arrived, I tried to distract myself by learning how to knit—another terrible idea. I already had quite a few blue blankets from my firstborn, so I chose to knit a pink blanket. I planned to finish the pink one and then knit a blue one. Knitting was not as easy as I had hoped. I bought a knitting book. I joined a knitting group. I watched knitting YouTube videos. And yet I still had to repeatedly frog my knitting (that means rip out my work, for all you non-knitters).

Halfway through the summer, it was clear I would be purling my way into the delivery room to finish this pink blanket. Forget even trying to knit a blue blanket. So my mother-in-law decided she would learn how to knit so she could make the blue blanket for me. Another horrible idea. I'm not even sure her knitting needles ever left their package. By the end of the summer, I had finally finished my pink blanket when my mother-in-law leaned over and said, "Don't worry, honey, if it's a boy, I'll just buy you a blanket." 'Cuz that's how we roll.

Fortunately for me, the baby, and the blanket, our second child was a girl! I wrapped our sweet baby Clarey up in that pink knitted blanket and snapped tons of photos to document the occasion. And you can bet I remind her every time I pull out that blanket how much sweat equity I spent carefully knitting and purling every row.

But no matter how much time and effort I put into knitting a baby blanket, it is nothing compared to the love, the tenderness, and the affection our heavenly Father put into creating us. Take a moment to reread Psalm 139:13–16.

Can you feel the adoration your heavenly Father has for you? He took great care in every detail when creating you. He knit you together. Nothing was hidden from Him. He ordained each and every one of your days. Does this sound like something He would do for someone who is a burden? No, only for His greatest treasure, His most awesome joy, and His biggest blessing.

If you could see as Jesus sees, through His lens of blessing, how would that change your view of yourself? Would you view yourself as fearfully and wonderfully made? Would you count each day as a blessing and a gift? Take some time to paint a picture in your head of what your life would look like if you stopped seeing yourself as a burden and started seeing yourself as a blessing. Now describe that life in words using the space provided.

_____

_____

_____

Elizabeth Oates

As Jesus Sees. . .Your Relationships

If you could see as Jesus sees, through His lens of blessing, how would it affect your relationships with others? My friend Beth recalls the time when she was recovering from her depression.

"Feeling better, I had started to walk in the early morning hours. The neighborhood I lived in was in close proximity to a lake. There was also a little bit of topography, and as I walked down the street toward the lake, the Big Dipper looked like it was sitting on the horizon on its side. I am very visual, and as I walked down the middle of the street in the dark, I would hold my arms over my head and talk to God. I prayed out loud for Him and the Holy Spirit to please give me whatever blessings I would need. . .just for today. I would pray this same prayer for each of my children and family members and others who were on my list. My friend Anne was always at the top!

"Then I would visualize these blessings 'pouring out' of the Big Dipper down through the atmosphere and into the top of my head. Every morning, the Big Dipper provided this incredible visualization for my prayers.

"One cloudy morning, as I walked down the street, the Big Dipper was not visible on the horizon. I stopped dead in my tracks and shouted out loud while standing in the middle of the street, 'This is what faith is about, believing in things you can't see. Okay God, I know that the Big Dipper is in the sky. I just can't see it. And I know that the blessings You have for me today will still pour out and flow down into me.' From this moment forward, I talked to everyone I knew about Big Dipper faith," Beth told me.

If you could see as Jesus sees, not through your lens of burden but through His lens of blessing, how would it affect your relationships? Would you be able to minister to others more effectively because you felt more confident about yourself? Would you respond with more compassion and empathy? Would you pray more passionately for others? Take a few moments to write down your thoughts on the next page.

As Jesus Sees. . .Your Community

If Beth's neighbor Anne had never walked across the street, would Beth have lived to share her story? We will never know. Think about someone in your community who might feel like a burden: the elderly woman, the inner-city kid, the unwed teen mom, your next-door neighbor. Now begin praying about how God wants you to minister to this person. If you can see others as Jesus sees them, as a blessing, loving those in your community will be as simple as breathing.

As Jesus Sees. . .Your Relationship with God

If you could see as Jesus sees, through His lens of blessing, how would it change your relationship with God? Could you stop living like Martha, sprinting frantically to and fro, always trying to create connection through activity instead of affinity? Could you instead live and love like Mary, unabashedly soaking up God's Word? Could you see yourself as a blessing to God, as His chosen daughter? Take a few moments to ponder this thought and journal any thoughts you have in the space provided.

Personal Reflection Questions

1. Elizabeth points out that in Matthew 19:13–15 Jesus takes time out for the little children, and He also takes time out for us because He is available and willing to meet with us every moment of every day. Do you take time out for Him? If so, what does that look like for you? If you do not take time out for Jesus, can you create a plan right now to begin spending one-on-one time with Him?

_____

_____

_____

_____

2. Do you have an early memory of feeling like a burden? If so, describe it here.

   - How old were you?
   - Where did you live?
   - Who made you feel like a burden?
   - What was the situation?
   - Do you still carry that feeling with you today?

_____

_____

_____

_____

_____

_____

3. Elizabeth writes, "God cannot change your past, but He wants to walk with you in your future." Now that you have read through this chapter, are you able to move beyond your past and see yourself not as a burden but as a blessing? If not, what will it take for you to accept this truth?

_____

_____

_____

_____

_____

4. What heavy baggage are you carrying that is rendering you immobile?

   • Are you ready to unpack it? If so, write a letter to God in the space provided, telling Him it's time to unpack your bag. Let Him know you will no longer see yourself as a burden; rather, you are ready to see yourself as Jesus sees you—as a blessing.

_____

_____

_____

_____

_____

_____

_____

5. Are there toxic people in your life who cause you to feel like a burden? If so, do you need to begin drawing healthy boundaries? List those boundaries in the space provided.

_____

_____

_____

_____

_____

_____

_____

_____

6. What lies does the enemy feed you that make you feel like a burden?

_____

_____

_____

_____

_____

_____

_____

_____

7. Elizabeth talks about making her friend Kelly feel like a burden. Is there someone in your life whom you are making feel like a burden? If so, what can you do to make that person feel like a blessing?

_____

_____

_____

_____

_____

_____

8. After reading Psalm 139:13–16, are you able to accept God's truth that you are a blessing and not a burden? If so, explain. If not, write a prayer asking God to help you accept this truth.

_____

_____

_____

_____

_____

_____

_____

_____

_____

Group Reflection Questions

1. Elizabeth points out that in Matthew 19:13–15 Jesus takes time out for the little children, and He also takes time out for us because He is available and willing to meet with us every moment of every day. Do you take time out for Him? If so, what does that look like for you? If you do not take time out for Jesus, can you create a plan right now to begin spending one-on-one time with Him?

2. Do you have an early memory of feeling like a burden? If so, describe it here.

    - How old were you?
    - Where did you live?
    - Who made you feel like a burden?
    - What was the situation?

3. Elizabeth writes, "God cannot change your past, but He wants to walk with you in your future." Now that you have read through this chapter, are you able to move beyond your past and see yourself not as a burden but as a blessing? If not, what will it take for you to accept this truth?

    - Do you still carry that feeling with you today?

4. What lies does the enemy feed you that make you feel like a burden?

5. Had you ever thought that you might make Jesus feel like a burden in your own life? Now that you have been introduced to the possibility, in what ways might you be doing this in your life?

Chapter 9

My Lens of Fear, His Lens of Bravery

As I mentioned, Brandon and I recently became foster parents. As I write this book, we are currently fostering a sweet baby girl. She came to our family when she was nine weeks old, and we immediately fell in love with her. Many people ask us, "When did you decide to become foster parents?" Truthfully, it was a decision thirteen years in the making.

When we first got married and lived in Dallas, Texas, we participated in various service projects and mission trips with Buckner International, a Dallas-based domestic and international adoption agency. We watched friends adopt through Buckner and had many conversations about the possibility of adopting one day. If we could have biological children, we knew we still felt called to adopt after one, maybe two, of our bio kids skipped off to school. I would probably adorn the nursery with baskets and bins I picked up from the Container Store, and we would live happily ever after. We had it all planned out, as most type A people do. And then God laughed.

Once we started trying to have children, our kids arrived in rapid succession. We popped out babies faster than Jiffy Pop Popcorn. By the time our oldest was four years old, we had three kids (surprise!), and we tabled all talks of adoption. We were up to our eyeballs in diapers, cribs, and crying. I was doing most of the crying.

We knew we needed to wait until our children were at an older stage of life before we could even think about adoption again. Over the years we approached the topic again, but it never felt like the right season.

Then, in the spring of 2014, during Lent, Brandon told me, "Every Thursday I'm going to fast and pray about some specific things. . .adoption is one of them."

"Awesome!" I told him. Brandon fasted. I prayed fast. That's the way it works in our house.

We set a date night at the end of Lent, which proved to be the most pivotal date night in the history of our marriage. At a picnic table, over a bowl of chips and salsa, we poured out our hearts. We talked about sacrifice and risk. We talked about the pros and cons of adoption (as if you can create a balance sheet for a child's life). We left that date knowing one thing for certain: we were gripped with fear. I feared many things:

- Sacrificing any sliver of freedom I had
- God giving us a child we could not handle
- Changing our family dynamics
- What people would think
- What people would say
- How people would react
- And, more than all of these things combined, I feared disobeying God.

Brandon wrestled with his own set of fears, including how to provide financially for a family of six and how to find time to pour into four children.

We knew our fears were selfish, yet we still left that dinner filled with tears and fears and lots of unanswered questions hanging in the air. We never imagined we would hear God's voice speak to us as loudly and clearly as He did when we went to church two days later.

Our executive pastor, Joey, preached a sermon titled "A Redeemed Legacy," in which he talked about "four behaviors that kill our family legacy." Those four behaviors include:

1. Fear
2. Isolationism
3. Selfishness
4. Worry

A few more Joey-isms from that Sunday morning sermon:

- "Fear prevents us from sacrificing."
- "If you're not taking risks for God, you succumb to fear."

- "We have to accept that the best decisions in life that result in true impact for our legacies are rarely the safest ones."
- "A lasting legacy is a unique one."

If I didn't know any better, I would have thought Joey had been sitting at the picnic table sharing our chips and salsa and eavesdropping on our date night.

Joey ended his sermon by asking everyone, "Where in your life is there fear? Where in your life screams selfishness? What in your life are you holding on to? My prayer is that you will let go of those things and let God break them up and turn them into fertile ground for a new legacy."

Brandon and I drove home and talked about the sermon. . .and we knew. We knew God was telling us to let go of our fear. We were so close to creating a family legacy, yet we knew we were succumbing to fear and isolationism and selfishness and worry. We knew God was calling us to adopt.

You might think that is the end of the story, but, like Jonah, I wanted to climb into the belly of a whale and just sit for three days. Actually, two weeks.

After Brandon and I made the decision to adopt, we made some phone calls. We talked to another couple we knew who had adopted both internationally and domestically. We spoke with a friend who worked at a local foster care and adoption agency. Then we prayed together. And separately. My individual prayer sounded a little different than our collective prayer.

Even though I had a heart for adoption for so many years, now that God was telling me to "go," I wanted to run as far away from my Nineveh as my scared little feet could carry me. So I prayed my Jonah-like prayer: "God, I know you are calling me to do this, but please don't make me do this. It's going to be hard and painful and messy, and I don't want to do it." I prayed over and over and over again for two weeks. I ran from what I knew God was calling me to do. And then one day I stopped running.

After two long weeks of tears and prayers and physical unrest—I surrendered my fears. My prayer changed from "I am scared; please don't make me do this" to "Here am I. Send me!" (Isaiah 6:8).

Common Fears

We all fear something in life: death, cancer, finances, job loss, failure, losing a loved one. Sometimes we can control our fears, yet other times our fears control us, paralyzing us and preventing us from living the life God calls us to live.

People have a variety of fears, including the following:
- flying
- public speaking
- the dark
- death or dying
- failure
- spiders
- commitment
- dentists
- needles
- being alone
- water
- clowns
- change
- crowds
- doctors
- being touched

When I think about all these fears that possess the power to kill and destroy our lives, I think about a verse our youngest son, Campbell, recently learned in preschool: "Be strong and courageous. Do not be afraid or terrified because of them, for the LORD your God goes with you; he will never leave you nor forsake you" (Deuteronomy 31:6). If we teach our children they should not succumb to fear but should instead cling to their Savior, shouldn't we do the same?

So what should we do when we feel afraid? The apostle Peter tells us, "Cast all your anxiety on him because he cares for you" (1 Peter 5:7). Run, don't walk, to your Savior. Pour out your heart to Him. Tell Him what weighs you down. He already knows. Tell Him anyway. Give a voice to your fears.

Think about this in context. If your child has a bad dream, would you rather she lie in bed all night, terrified, crying all by herself? Or would you rather she tiptoe into your room and tell you every detail? Then you can gently walk her back into her room, tuck her into bed, and sit with her as you rub her back and reassure her that you are her protector and rescuer. I vote for option B. And so does Jesus. He longs for us to run to Him, to pour out our souls to Him, and to allow Him to calm our fears with His truth.

Not-So-Brave Peter

In the book of Matthew, we read about Jesus and His disciples and a dark, windy night out on a boat. I don't have aquaphobia (the fear of water) but this scene scares me already. The disciples are hanging out in the boat while Jesus prays on a mountaintop. "Shortly before dawn Jesus went out to them, walking on the lake. When the disciples saw him walking on the lake, they were terrified. 'It's a ghost,' they said, and cried out in fear. But Jesus immediately said to them: 'Take courage! It is I. Don't be afraid.' 'Lord, if it's you,' Peter replied, 'tell me to come to you on the water.' 'Come,' he said" (Matthew 14:25–29).

Now, you would think that when God in the flesh tells you to "take courage" and "come" that would give you all the confidence you need to obey. Peter does obey. For a split second, Peter feels brave—so brave that he walks on water, just like Jesus. But then what happens? Peter stops seeing himself through Jesus' lens of bravery and starts seeing himself through His own lens of fear.

"But when he saw the wind, he was afraid and, beginning to sink, cried out, 'Lord, save me!' Immediately Jesus reached out his hand and caught him. 'You of little faith,' he said, 'why did you doubt?' And when they climbed into the boat, the wind died down. Then those who were in the boat worshiped him, saying, 'Truly you are the Son of God'" (Matthew 14:30–33).

It is almost as if Peter wears blinders when he first steps out of the boat. He sees Jesus and knows exactly where he should walk. But the moment Peter casts aside the blinders, fear overwhelms him.

The Voice translates verse 31: "Immediately Jesus reached for Peter and caught him. Jesus: O you of little faith. Why did you doubt and dance back and forth between following Me and heeding fear?" Can't you just visualize Peter dancing back and forth between faith and fear? Between confidence and doubt? Between trusting Jesus and trusting himself? Sadly, isn't that how we all live life—one minute seeing ourselves through Jesus' lens of bravery, believing we can conquer the world, the next minute seeing ourselves through our own lens of fear, cowering to every negative comment and glance?

Not-So-Brave Peter teaches us several things. First, he teaches us that life is not static; God always challenges us and pushes us to new frontiers. Personally, I like change. But some people enjoy the steady rhythm of a quieter, more routine life. If you fall into this category, let me encourage you with this point of view: by resisting God's call on your life, you will trade some of the greatest, most life-giving adventures for mere monotony and predictability. Every time I look at our sweet foster baby, I think, "I can't believe I almost missed out on this. I almost missed out on *her*." And for what? To play it safe? To maintain predictability? Doesn't sound like a great trade, does it?

Second, Peter teaches us that in the very moment we think God is about to fail us, that is the moment He shows up. Every. Single. Time. How many times have you accepted a call from the Lord but when the going gets tough, you second-guess everything? Maybe God asked you to start a nonprofit and then your major donor bailed two months after you launched. Maybe God asked you to mentor a high school student but she's making some poor choices and distancing herself from you.

Maybe your child was born with a medical condition that has robbed you of your time, money, and energy. Now what? This isn't what you signed up for. This wasn't the deal. You're not this brave. You're not this strong. In fact, you're scared. You're terrified. You can't handle this. You're not up for the task!

Exactly.

God knows you cannot handle the stress and strain that life demands, which is why He always shows up. Just as He did for Peter. Bravery isn't about making deals. Bravery is about showing up, even when we are scared. Especially when we are scared. Bravery is about showing up when no one else will. Bravery is about leading others when the waves are high and the night is dark and all you want to do is sit in the boat but Jesus says, "Come." So you do.

Finally, Peter teaches us that the moment we stop looking through Jesus' lens of bravery and start looking through our own lens of fear, that is the very moment in which we sink. Before Peter yielded to his fear, he was accomplishing far more than he ever could have imagined—he was walking on water! And then he remembered his own immortality, his own limitations, his own imperfections. . .and he sank.

Has God ever given you an assignment or task that you carried out with great vigor and excitement until that moment in which you paused long enough to think, *What am I doing? People must think I'm crazy. What if I fail?* And then you did. You failed. You crashed and burned, not because you were doomed to fail, but because you looked through your lens of fear instead of Jesus' lens of bravery.

When we live on mission with Jesus, we must never look around at what everyone else is doing. We don't have the luxury of worrying about what other people think or say or do. Like Peter when he took his first step off the boat, we must put on our blinders and forge ahead, thinking of one person, and only one person: Jesus.

Cheering Section

What if Peter had had a cheering section? What if the guys in the boat had yelled, "Come on, Peter! You can do it! We know you can! You're doing it! You're walking on water! You're almost there! Don't look down!" Okay, maybe that last part would have been the wrong thing to say, but you get the idea. What if Peter's band of brothers had encouraged him at the most pivotal moment in his life? Maybe then he would have clung to his bravery instead of sinking into the ocean.

I have a tremendous fear of heights. I got sick when I tried parasailing on a family vacation. I passed out on a helicopter ride on my honeymoon. Heights and I are not friends. It's common, I know. But it's real. Don't judge. In fact, according to a recent survey by Chapman University, heights rank second in fears, just behind public speaking.[1] I am happy to report I do not possess the fears of clowns or zombies.

I remember when I was a sophomore in high school and hanging out with my best friend, Sarah. Her uncle ran a sports camp for youth, so one beautiful spring weekend Sarah's family took us out there for the day. I didn't grow up attending camp, so the entire experience was foreign to me. Her uncle, unaware of my fear, suggested we try the pamper pole. I, unaware of what the pamper pole entailed, heartily agreed.

If you are camp virgin like I was, allow me to let you in on a little secret. The pamper pole is a twenty-foot high pole about the diameter of a telephone pole. Sane, rational people actually choose—of their own free will—to climb to the top. You know, just for fun. Then, once you're at the top, you stand there looking down! At the ground! I think you are supposed to admire God's creation, but who can focus on God's bounty when you are standing twenty feet from your death? After pausing a moment to hyperventilate, your camp counselor, or grim reaper, as I like to call him, tells you to jump—*jump*! You have to jump off this death trap and try to catch a trapeze-like PVC-pipe, swing for a moment, just for kicks, then let go so the counselor can slowly (I use the term *slowly* loosely, because it actually feels like you are falling at warp speed) lower you to the ground. So as not to mar the camp's reputation, I should mention that participants always wear a harness and helmet, but that is of little consolation for people with undiagnosed acrophobia.

My friend Sarah eagerly conquered the pamper pole. Her brother followed, no problem. Then it was my turn. They suited me up. To say I was shaking would be an understatement. I wanted to back out. I tried to back out. But I had this entire cheering section telling me I could do it. Sarah's parents, aunt, uncle, cousins, grandparents—everyone—were there clapping, shouting words of encouragement, telling me I was strong and capable and I could do this. I was just hoping I wouldn't pee in my harness.

I slowly climbed up the pamper pole, feeling the entire thing shake as I made my way to the top. When I was halfway up the pole, someone yelled, "Don't look down." Well, you know what you do when someone tells you *not* to do something—you do it. I looked down. Big mistake. Twenty feet is even higher than it sounds. I felt my eyes water with tears. Acrophobia is no joke. But I didn't want to disappoint them, so I kept climbing.

Finally, after a few pauses along the way, I made it to the top. But I still had to stand directly on top. In order to do that, I had to hoist myself to a standing position with nothing to hold on to. I wanted to climb down, but I knew Sarah's family wasn't about to let me get away with that. After a very slow press on top of the pole, I did it. I was standing! My knees were shaking like two maracas, but I was standing! Now there was only one thing left to do.

"Jump!" they all yelled. The last thing I wanted to do was jump to my death. What if the harness didn't work? Sure, it worked for Sarah and her brother, but what if I was that girl who ended up on the nightly news? I can hear the headlines now: Tragic Accident at Hill Country Camp: Girl Soaring through the Air Now Soars into Heaven.

Their cheers snapped me back into reality. "You can do it, Elizabeth! Just jump. Reach for the bar!" I eventually jumped. I didn't reach the bar, but I also didn't die. Winning! The harness didn't break, and I also didn't pee in it. Mission accomplished. And I lived to tell the tale.

If I had seen myself through my own lens, I would have seen nothing but a girl who was afraid of heights—a girl who was incompetent, incapable, and untalented. But God gave me an awesome cheering section that day that allowed me to work through my fear of heights and see myself through Jesus' lens of talent. We all need a cheering section to tell us that we are competent, capable, worthy, and talented.

Have you ever had anyone cheer you on? Have your family members or friends ever told you that you are smart enough, talented enough, capable enough to accomplish your goals, overcome your fears, and go after your dreams? Without a cheering section, it is difficult to make our dreams a reality.

I want you to know, friend, that God believes in you. He is your cheering section. He says that you are talented and capable and competent, even when the world says that you are not.

The apostle Paul tells us, "I know what it is to be in need, and I know what it is to have plenty. I have learned the secret of being content in any and every situation, whether well fed or hungry, whether living in plenty or in want. I can do all this through him who gives me strength" (Philippians 4:12–13).

Where was Paul when he wrote this letter? Historians believe he was living in a Roman prison. I am guessing Paul didn't have much of a cheering section there. Yet he wrote to encourage his fellow believers anyway. He wrote about contentment and strength. Paul saw himself through Jesus' lens and knew he had the strength to carry out Jesus' mission no matter where that took him. You have the same Holy Spirit living in you that Paul had living in him. This means you have the same strength. Anything God calls you to do, you can accomplish, just as Paul did.

Fear and Inaction

I never sit still. I am a stay-at-home mom who never stays home. I am on the move and on the go. Last year Brandon and I bought his and her Fitbits to track our activity (Yes!) and sleep (Yeah, right). Brandon started the competition with a little trash talk, "I know you're gonna beat me in activity, but I'm gonna beat you in sleep." I think we both know where our strengths lie. For me it's activity. For him it's inactivity. We've made peace with it.

For the majority of my stay-at-home mom years, I have lived a double life: writer and yoga instructor. I spent many years overextending myself and trying to find balance in an unbalanced life.

In the spring of 2014, the same season we decided to pursue adoption through foster care, I finally paused long enough to listen to God's voice. He told me to stop chasing both dreams. It wasn't possible anymore. If I was going to pursue writing, I had to be all in. So I listened. Not only did I listen, but I mustered up all the courage I could find and let go of my yoga life: my classes, my clients, my everything.

At first I was filled with fear. What if I fail at writing? What if I regret my decision? What if I look foolish? But once I submitted to the decision, I experienced such peace.

I can't say that taking a break from yoga was easy. The months following that decision proved to be some of the most difficult I ever experienced, and I second-guessed my decision—and God's call—many times.

I wish I could say my faith was solid, unwavering, faultless. I am the one writing this book, after all. But apparently I am also the one who needs to read it. Not only did my faith waver, but I succumbed to fear daily. I feared so many things that I no longer felt active or energized or brave. Instead, for months when I crawled in bed at night, I was emotionally and spiritually spent.

Many days I leaned on this verse: "The LORD will fight for you; you need only to be still" (Exodus 14:14). I didn't feel brave or strong or courageous. I felt weak and scared and tired. All I could do was be still and allow God to fight for me. And sometimes that is all He asks of us. Sometimes seeing ourselves through Jesus' lens of bravery means being still.

As Jesus Sees. . .You

Let's take a few moments for self-reflection. What do you fear in life? Use the space below to list some of your fears:

_____

_____

_____

_____

_____

How would Jesus' lens of bravery help you conquer your fears? Again, use the list from above, but now write how Jesus' lens of bravery would help you conquer each individual fear.

_____

_____

_____

_____

_____

_____

_____

If you could see yourself as Jesus sees you, through His lens of bravery, how would it change you?

_____

_____

_____

_____

_____

_____

_____

As Jesus Sees. . .Your Relationships

One night while on a date, Brandon and I were reminiscing about college. We are college sweethearts, and although he is two years older than me, we had a lot of mutual friends. I told him that when we were in college, girls saw him as the nice, small-town, no-drama, easy-going, easy-to-get-along-with guy. Much like he is today. No surprise there.

"What did guys think of me in college?" I asked casually, pretending I didn't really care. As if. Ha!

"Um, I don't think I want to play this game," he said cautiously, knowing what can of worms he was about to open. I sensed his hesitation.

"Oh, we're playing it!" I said. "Game on!" In retrospect, I don't recommend this kind of table talk, ladies. Unless you want your one kid-free date night of the year to end poorly.

"Umm." He paused. Never a good sign. "Elizabeth. . .fun girl. Hard to get to know on a deeper level."

"*Whaaaaat?*" I yelled. "What are you talking about? I am Miss Deep Waters!" I could not believe what I was hearing. Me? Shallow? Hard to get to know? I am an open book! Clearly. . .I am *writing* a book!

"So who are all these people who think I am hard to get to know? I want names!"

"Um, obviously this was a bad idea," Brandon said, backing off.

"No, I think it was a *great* idea," I retorted. I think we can all read between the lines here. If this were an episode of *Real Housewives of McLennan County*, this would be the pre-table flipping scene.

"I think you should just let it go," he said calmly (and that was before the movie *Frozen*—he is so ahead of his time).

"No way! I am not hard to get to know. What do you want to know? Just ask me. I'll tell you anything."

And, of course, Brandon just sat there with that I'm-so-calm-and-clearly-you-need-a-Xanax smirk on his face, just like always. "I don't need to know anything. I already know everything. I'm just saying that in college you were a little hard to read sometimes."

"Whatever. People knew me. I had friends, tons of friends. And dates too. No serious boyfriend, but I definitely dated."

"Exactly," my attorney husband said, as if he had just won his biggest court case ever. He sat back in his chair, arms folded, as if to make his point even clearer. Worst. Date. Ever.

So maybe relationships aren't my strong suit (hello. . .Darth Vader!). But I am a work in progress. Aren't we all?

Relationships require a certain level of risk and vulnerability, the ability and willingness to balance heartache and loss with joy and thanksgiving. If we see ourselves through our lens of fear, we lack the ability to connect with others emotionally and spiritually. But if we see ourselves through Jesus' lens of bravery, we are able to let others peer deep into our emotions and us into theirs.

Thinking about your relationships, both past and present, how does your lens of fear affect your authentic connections with people? Does it cause you to distance yourself? Put up walls of protection? Or do you open yourself up to the possibility of pain in exchange for the likelihood of joy?

Take some time to consider how fear affects your relationships, friendships, and connections with other people. Use the space provided to write down your answer.

_____

_____

_____

_____

_____

_____

_____

Now pause to consider this question: If you could stop seeing yourself through your lens of fear and start seeing yourself through Jesus' lens of bravery, how would that change your relationships? How would overcoming your fears help you connect more with people? How would overcoming your fears help you become more vulnerable with people in your life? How would overcoming your fears help you form more authentic relationships with others?

_____

_____

_____

_____

_____

_____

_____

As Jesus Sees. . .Your Community

One of my all-time favorite books is *The Giver* by Lois Lowry. While I can't keep up with most of what Carter reads, I do know he has not read *The Giver*. I am just not ready for my nine-year-old to read about "the stirrings." I am clinging to his innocence as long as I can.

In *The Giver*, when every child reaches the age of twelve, he or she is selected for an assignment, or job. Jonas is selected to be the Receiver, meaning he will receive all the colors, experiences, and memories that have been locked away and kept secret from society for generations. One thematic question raised in the book is, do we have a right to decide how much pain and loss people can bear?

Spoiler alert: At the end of the book, Jonas bravely rescues a baby boy, Gabriel, destined for "Elsewhere," aka death. Why does Jonas make this brave yet risky decision? Because Jonas has tasted life. He knows more than his community knows and sees more than his people see. He can't unknow or unsee the truth. So he leaves his community forever to give himself and Gabriel a chance to experience a true, authentic, new life.

How many of us know and see the truth in color, like Jonas, yet continue living our lives in black and white? We know about genocide, prostitution, child hunger, and elder neglect. We are privy to home-lessness and cyber bullying. We are educated about abuse, addiction, marginalization, and sex trafficking. We know these issues are not just prevalent in third world countries. They are five and ten miles down the road—maybe even next door. Yet how many of us spend more time at playgroups, book clubs, and PTA meetings than we do caring for the least of these?

Why do we shy away from those Jesus calls us to serve? Didn't He say, "It is not the healthy who need a doctor, but the sick. I have not come to call the righteous, but sinners" (Mark 2:17)?

- Do we fear the time it might take to serve those in need?
- Do we fear the emotional energy we will expend?
- Do we fear overloading our schedules?

- Do we fear what others will think when we get involved with those who don't look like us, act like us, or think like us?

If you could see as Jesus sees, through His lens of bravery, how would it change your community? Could you rescue a child, like Jonas did? Could you speak up for those who have no voice? Could you see beyond your own four walls to the needs of those around you? Take some time to pray through how God is asking you to be brave in your community, then journal your thoughts in the space provided.

_____

_____

_____

_____

_____

_____

_____

_____

_____

_____

_____

_____

_____

_____

_____

As Jesus Sees. . .Your Relationship with God

Sometimes we fear a situation because we are left alone without a wingman. But God promises we are never truly by ourselves. "Have I not commanded you? Be strong and courageous. Do not be afraid; do not be discouraged, for the LORD your God will be with you wherever you go" (Joshua 1:9).

If you could see as Jesus sees, through His lens of bravery, how would that change your relationship with your Creator? Would you cast aside feelings of fear and doubt, knowing that God is always present in your life? Take a moment to reflect on this truth and how it applies to your life today. Then journal any thoughts you might have.

_____

_____

_____

_____

_____

_____

_____

_____

_____

_____

_____

_____

_____

Personal Reflection Questions

1. Elizabeth's pastor, Joey, challenged his congregation by asking:
    - "Where in your life is there fear?"
    - "Where in your life screams selfishness?"
    - "What in your life are you holding on to?"

    For Elizabeth and Brandon, these were the very questions that helped them abandon their fears and pursue foster care. Can you answer those questions honestly regarding your own life?

    _____

    _____

    _____

    _____

    _____

    _____

    _____

2. Elizabeth provides a long list of common fears. Do any of these resonate with you? If so, which ones?

    - How can you rely on God to overcome these fears?

    _____

    _____

    _____

    _____

    _____

3. In the story of Peter walking on the water, Peter teaches us three things:
      - Life is not static; God will always challenge us and push us to new frontiers.
      - When we think God is not going to come through, He always does.
      - The moment we stop looking through Jesus' lens of bravery and start looking through our own lens of fear, is the very moment in which we will sink.

   Which of these three lessons impacted you the most? Explain.

   _____

   _____

   _____

   _____

   _____

   _____

4. Who is in your cheering section? If you don't have someone, commit to praying that God will provide someone in your life who will cheer you on and support you.

   _____

   _____

   _____

   _____

5. How would overcoming your fears and seeing yourself through Jesus' lens of bravery change your community and your world?

- How would you be able to influence people in a different way?
- How would you be able to engage in your community in a different, more meaningful way?

_____

_____

_____

_____

_____

_____

_____

_____

_____

_____

_____

_____

_____

_____

_____

_____

Group Reflection Questions

1. Elizabeth's pastor, Joey, challenged his congregation by asking:
   - "Where in your life is there fear?"
   - "Where in your life screams selfishness?"
   - "What in your life are you holding on to?"

   For Elizabeth and Brandon, these were the very questions that helped them abandon their fears and pursue foster care. Can you answer those questions honestly regarding your own life?

2. Elizabeth provides a long list of common fears. Do any of these resonate with you? If so, which ones?

   - How are you relying on God to overcome these fears?

3. In the story of Peter walking on the water, Peter teaches us three things:
   - Life is not static; God will always challenge us and push us to new frontiers.
   - When we think God is not going to come through, He always does.
   - The moment we stop looking through Jesus' lens of bravery and start looking through our own lens of fear, that is the very moment in which we will sink.

   Which of these three lessons impacted you the most? Explain.

4. Who is in your cheering section? If you don't have someone, commit to pray that God would provide someone in your life who will cheer you on and support you.

5. You were asked to list some things you fear. If you are comfortable sharing, take a few moments to do that here.

   - If you could see yourself as Jesus sees you, through His lens of bravery, how would it change you?

6. How does fear affect your relationships, friendships, and connections with other people?

   - If you could stop seeing yourself through your lens of fear and start seeing through Jesus' lens of bravery, how would it change your relationships?
   - How would overcoming your fears help you connect more with people?
   - How would overcoming your fears help you become more vulnerable with people in your life? How would overcoming your fears help you form more authentic relationships with others?

7. How would overcoming your fears and seeing yourself through Jesus' lens of bravery change your community and your world?

   - How would you be able to influence people in a different way?
   - How would you be able to engage in your community in a different, more meaningful way?

Chapter 10

My Lens of Condemnation, His Lens of Forgiveness

We all know *that* mom. The one we put on a pedestal. The one who does everything right. She feeds her kids organic foods, sends them to private school, takes them to the museum to study fine art, and never loses her patience. I have one such uber-mom friend, Katy. I have seriously thought about asking Katy to raise *my* children. Maybe she could even raise me while she's at it. Please, Katy? Take me to your magical mom world and teach me your ways.

I remember one time Katy's oldest daughter, who was around three or four years old at the time, committed some minor offense against her younger sister. "Emma, say you're sorry," Katy told her.

"I sorry," Emma squeaked out in her sweetest voice. But the scene didn't end there.

"Margaret," my friend, Katy, said to her youngest daughter, "say, 'I forgive you.'"

"I fogive you," Margaret replied, barely taking her thumb out of her mouth.

Um, what just happened? What was this exchange I had just witnessed? I thought we were just settling an argument over crayons, not preparing them for lifelong conflict resolution. Katy must have picked up on my perplexity. She looked over at me and explained.

"Saying, 'I'm sorry,' is easy. Extending and receiving forgiveness is much more difficult."

Growing up, my own brother and I rarely apologized to each other, and I know we never uttered the words, "I forgive you," when we were mere toddlers. My theology and my attitude toward forgiveness changed that day at Katy's house.

What about you? Maybe you need to forgive someone for past abuse, abandonment, childhood bullying, or some other act committed against you. Maybe you need to forgive yourself for your past mistakes, yet you don't know how because no one has modeled true forgiveness. Maybe no one has ever said to you, "I'm sorry," "I forgive you," or "Will you forgive me?"

Rest assured, my friend. Jesus is our model. He forgives people who do not deserve forgiveness. He loves people who hate Him. He extends mercy and grace where there should be none. And He wants you to see as He sees—through His lens of forgiveness. So let's dive in deep, shall we?

If We Could Forgive as Jesus Forgives

What exactly is forgiveness? It was a deep theological truth for such a tiny tot. And yet Emma understood it, even more so than many adults I know. In a nutshell, forgiveness is canceling a debt. If a person owes us something, we tell her she owes us nothing. We cancel, or forgive, her debt. Forgiveness also means:
- Releasing resentment you have built up toward another person (Proverbs 19:11).
- Accepting the past for what it is and moving forward into the future (Jeremiah 29:11).
- Seeking the best for the other person (1 Corinthians 13:4–6).
- Trusting God to dole out justice (Romans 12:19).

We see a powerful act of forgiveness on Jesus' final trek to the hill called Golgotha—a journey so painful, so tiresome, so excruciating that He could not shuffle one more step while shouldering His own heavy cross. The guards stop. They peer into the crowd. They spot a random man. No one significant. Just Simon from Cyrene. He'll do. They pull him out of the mob and force him to carry Jesus' cross the rest of the way to Golgotha. . .to the Skull. When the entourage arrives, the cowardly soldiers nail Jesus' hands and feet to His cross, then mercilessly hoist it upright.

Scripture reads: "Two other men, both criminals, were also led out with him to be executed. When they came to the place called the Skull, they crucified him there, along with the criminals—one on his right, the other on his left. Jesus said, 'Father, forgive them, for they do not know what they are doing.' And they divided up his clothes by casting lots" (Luke 23:32–34). As commoners catapult insults and jeers, the King of the Jews gently offers mercy and forgiveness. . .and forever changes the landscape of our world.

Although this is not the first time Jesus talks about forgiveness, this scene certainly sets the tone for how we are to approach forgiveness in our own relationships, ministry, love, and life. When people insult us, Jesus tells us to forgive. When they question our credentials and identity, Jesus tells us to forgive. When they seek to destroy our spirits and souls, Jesus tells us to forgive. When they take our possessions, Jesus tells us to forgive. When they try to isolate us, Jesus tells us to forgive. When they hate us, Jesus tells us to forgive. When they condemn us, what else are we to do but forgive?

If We Could Forgive Others

"But that's Jesus," you might argue. "I can't forgive like He forgives. I don't have His strength, His purity, His confidence, His faith. I'm not God in flesh. I'm just me." You're wrong. You do have Jesus' strength. If you have accepted Jesus as your Savior and you have faith in Him, you can move mountains (Matthew 17:20). You can, my friend!

"But you don't know anything about me. You don't know what's been done to me. You don't know what I have lived through," you might object. You're right. I don't know your story, but I wish I did. Oh, how I wish I could meet you for coffee and listen as you pour out your heart, share your pain, your disappointments, your hurts, your dreams, your ideas, and your hopes. I admit, I am not sitting right in front of you, but our God is! And He longs to infiltrate your soul, to pierce your heart, to change your life so that forgiveness trumps all other options when it comes to our relationships.

Forgiveness is a choice. Much like love. And it does not always come naturally or easily. When Jesus hung on the cross, He made a conscious decision to appeal to His Father on behalf of His persecutors—on behalf of you and me. Every day we have this same choice. Will we stay cemented in bitterness? Will we stay entangled in condemnation? Or will we find freedom and joy in forgiving others?

Corrie ten Boom, born in 1892 in the Netherlands, is best known for her service to the Jews during World War II. She and her family harbored approximately eight hundred Jews to protect them from being arrested by Nazi authorities. On February 24, 1944, a fellow Dutch citizen betrayed her family. Corrie and five family members were arrested and imprisoned that day. Sadly, only Corrie and her sister Nollie survived. After she was released from a Jewish concentration camp, Corrie ten Boom started a worldwide ministry to tell people about Jesus' love. She later wrote about her World War II experience in the book *The Hiding Place*.

She writes, "Even as the angry, vengeful thoughts boiled through me, I saw the sin of them. Jesus Christ had died for this man; was I going to ask for more? Lord Jesus, I prayed, forgive me and help me to forgive him. . . . Jesus, I cannot forgive him. Give me your forgiveness. . . . And so I discovered that it is not on our forgiveness any more than on our goodness that the world's healing hinges, but on His. When He tells us to love our enemies, He gives along with the command, the love itself."[1]

So, revisiting your objection, "But that's Jesus. I can't forgive like He forgives." You're right. You are not Jesus. I am not Jesus. Corrie ten Boom was not Jesus. Even so, the apostle Paul assures us, "Do you not know that you are God's temple and that God's Spirit dwells in you?" (1 Corinthians 3:16 ESV). If the Holy Spirit lives within each of us, then He gives us the supernatural ability—the same ability Jesus possessed—to forgive others. Whether we tap into the power of the Holy Spirit and actually use it to forgive others is our choice.

Do you feel God calling you to forgive someone, yet you can't bring yourself to take that step? Do you know what is holding you back?

Many reasons exist why we choose not to forgive others:

- We think forgiveness gives them permission to continue hurting us.
- We think forgiveness excuses or condones their behavior.
- We think withholding forgiveness punishes our offender.
- We think forgiveness means we must forget what was done to us.
- We think that if we forgive, then we must reconcile.

Forgiveness is none of the above. Forgiveness is the act of modeling what Jesus did that dreadful, beautiful day on the cross. Forgiveness is simply a gift we give ourselves—a gift to walk in freedom and truth and joy and light. Forgiveness is a response to live obediently with Jesus instead of dancing a never-ending dance with the devil.

Scripture tells us, "For if you forgive other people when they sin against you, your heavenly Father will also forgive you. But if you do not forgive others their sins, your Father will not forgive your sins" (Matthew 6:14–15). If we want to live according to God's Word, forgiveness is not an option. It is a command, designed by God, for our mental, emotional, physical, and spiritual health, and for the health of our community. When we forgive, we thrive; and when we thrive, everyone around us flourishes.

If We Could Forgive Ourselves

Maybe forgiving other people is not what holds you back from living a spiritually rich life—maybe you need to forgive yourself. Do you feel tethered to past mistakes and regrets that you can't seem to shake? Have you spent years running away from your sins, only to look back and find yourself just two feet from the starting line?

In our house we offer our children lots of "rephrases" and "redos." For instance, we often tell our children, "Please rephrase that," when they speak disrespectfully, or "Let's try that again with respect," when they do something rude or mean to a sibling.

Oh, how I wish life gave me the chance to rephrase my words or redo my actions. But once I speak impatiently to a store clerk or ignore my neighbor's needs, my words and actions float around like snow flurries in the great snow globe of life mixed up with everyone else's lyrics, chattering, and activities. Unfortunately, life is not as forgiving or kind as it is in the Oates household. I can't simply remove my ugly snow from the snow globe. Once I speak or act, it's stuck out in the universe for eternity.

Thankfully, this is not the end of the story. I can examine my "Do-Over Wish List" and make amends with another person or with myself. And so can you. Have you said something you wish you could take back? Done something you wish you could do over? Maybe your "Do-Over Wish List" consists of one of the following:

- A job you wish you had taken
- An adulterous affair you regret
- A yelling match with your child you wish you had handled differently
- Harsh words said to your parent that you wish you could take back
- Emotional support you wish you had given to your spouse
- An important conversation you wish you had had with a friend
- Serious debt you put your family in that you regret
- An addiction you succumbed to once again

All of these things are decisions we make in life that, in hindsight, we wish we had handled differently.

For instance, one day my kids begged me to help them host a lemonade stand. Not to brag, but our house claims prime real estate in the neighborhood when it comes to lemonade stands. Location, location, location. If you set up shop at 5:15 p.m., you hit everyone arriving home from work. *Cha-ching!* Clearly we have figured out how to work the system. It was a cool 75 degrees that particular day, and Dad would be working late that night, so I knew we had some time to kill. I agreed to my little capitalists' business venture, deep down knowing I was tired and outnumbered, and these two factors alone meant our lemonade stand was a recipe for disaster.

Our family adventure quickly turned into a neighborhood activity when lots of little "helpers" swarmed onto the scene. With my daughter outnumbered by her brothers and their friends, her happiness vanished into frustration and tears. Our lemonade stand quickly turned sour. My patience ran thin, my words became curt, and I morphed from June Cleaver into Cruella De Vil. I closed up shop and sent everyone home, angry with myself for not remaining more patient.

I thought about that lemonade stand for days, unable to forgive myself. I knew I had disappointed my kids and their friends. But deep down, there was a bigger issue lying underneath the surface of sticky lemonade. What really frustrated me was that I was not the kind of mom I wanted to be—the mom I imagined in my head. The mom who keeps it together at all times. The mom who never loses her patience. The mom who goes with the flow. The mom who seamlessly embraces an army of kids at her house. The mom I portray on social media. A few days out of the year, I am this mom. But on this day, I wasn't, and I couldn't forgive myself.

Fast-forward one week. I attended a parenting conference for foster and adoptive parents called "Empowered to Connect" with Dr. Karyn Purvis speaking. I often feel like a failure when I attend parenting conferences because I focus on the majority of the things I am *not* implementing instead of the few things I am doing well. So I engage in negative self-talk and refuse to forgive myself for all my mistakes. I focus on the past, refusing to find hope in the future. (Um, maybe I need to read *If You Could See as Jesus Sees*.) Yet, in His mercy, God revealed one truth to me at this conference: we will never do everything perfectly, but we can do a few things really well. And over time these few things will add up to big results.

I think my type A mentality is often what prevents me from forgiving myself. Maybe you have the same problem. We expect perfection. We expect instant results and miracles when, in reality, God only wants our willingness to submit to Him. Out of our submission flows transformation. Paul writes, "Do not conform to the pattern of this world, but be transformed by the renewing of your mind. Then you will be able to test and approve what God's will is—his good, pleasing and perfect will" (Romans 12:2). Transformation doesn't happen overnight. It is a process, much like a butterfly emerging from its cocoon.

For some of us, perfection is not the issue. Maybe it is the pain of our past mistakes that is just too great. Maybe the consequences of our sin are too far reaching and we don't know how to rectify our actions: the affair that broke up our marriage, the argument that left our extended family disconnected, the gossip train that resulted in severed relationships. How could anyone, especially God, ever forgive us for messing up our own lives and the lives of others?

Because He already has, my friend. The day God watched His only Son die on the cross was the day He forgave you.

No amount of self-loathing, no amount of bitterness, no amount of you staying stuck in your place of condemnation will change this truth. God loves you. God forgives you. And He wants you to forgive yourself. He longs for you to see yourself the way He sees you—through His lens of forgiveness.

So what prevents you from forgiving yourself? Why do you stay stuck in bitterness rather than moving forward in joy? Why do you see yourself through your lens of condemnation instead of through Jesus' lens of forgiveness? Below is a list of reasons why we don't forgive ourselves:

- We don't believe we deserve forgiveness. Holding on to our crime is the lifelong penance we must pay.
- We think other people will judge us and think we are not taking our sin seriously if we forgive ourselves and move on.
- We want to feel the severity and consequences of the decision we made.

All of these reasons for self-condemnation are not founded in God's Word but are lies fabricated by the enemy to keep us shackled in chains of despair, doubt, and grief. So how can we move past these deceptions toward hope and healing and ultimately forgive ourselves?

- Accept that you are a flawed person who will make mistakes, just as all human beings do.
- Let go of the past and accept that you cannot change it. Focus on the future.
- Let go of other people's expectations. Live according to God's standards and no one else's.
- Make amends (if possible) with the offended party. Then confess your sins to God.
- Accept that God has forgiven you; therefore you can forgive yourself.

Don't let condemnation rob you of the joy Christ has to offer. Jesus wants you to live an abundant life in Him. No fruit will grow, however, if we live in a spiritual drought of bitterness and despair.

If We Could Forgive and Not Forget

We have often heard the saying, "Forgive and forget." The problem is, unless we suffer from a case of amnesia, we will never truly forget our sins or the sins committed against us. Guess what? This is not entirely bad news! Remembering our sins helps us avoid temptation. It also helps us remember where we were in our spiritual walk and where we do not want to go. Finally, it reminds us of God's forgiveness and helps us to forgive others. Given these truths, should we try to remember our sins? This seems contradictory from what the Bible teaches.

The prophet Jeremiah recorded God's words about forgiveness: "'No longer will they teach their neighbor, or say to one another, "Know the Lord," because they will all know me, from the least of them to the greatest,' declares the Lord. 'For I will forgive their wickedness and will remember their sins no more'" (Jeremiah 31:34).

When God says He will "remember their sins no more," He does not really mean He will forget the Israelites' sins. He is saying that He will not bring up their sins in a negative way. He will not keep score.

Our children love to keep score. Any time our older son wants to play on the Wii, he says, "I should get to play because Campbell got to play on the Wii already." My response? "We don't keep score." We don't keep track of good things or bad things, rights or wrongs. We simply don't keep score. I would drive my already insane mind even crazier if I tried to keep the exact count of playdates and Popsicles and screen time each of my children accrued. Therefore, I work toward "close enough" and call it a day. Beyond that, I call out, "We don't keep score."

The good news is, God doesn't keep score either. When we make a mistake, He doesn't bring up the past. *Elizabeth, I can't believe you lost your temper again! Even after you lost your patience at the lemonade stand last week. Have you learned nothing? That's a double sin, which means double prayers and asking for double forgiveness.* No. That's not the way our God works. So why do we work that way?

Before continuing this chapter, let's pause for a moment and work through appendix D on page 252 to help us tackle sin and forgiving and forgetting. Sometimes people sin against us. We think we have forgiven them until something else happens. This second or third or whatever offense stirs up old emotions, and we wonder whether we truly did forgive the offender.

This "If We Could Forgive and Not Forget" chart helps us work through an offense committed against us. It helps us mentally process the situation, forgive the person, and put the incident behind us once and for all. If something occurs that triggers a memory about the event, we can simply turn to our chart, read our notes, and remind ourselves of the powerful work of forgiveness God helped us complete. We will know that we have forgiven that person and moved on. If a new event occurs, we can add on to our chart, journal our feelings, work through forgiveness, and refer back to the chart as needed.

We will use the same process for situations where we need to forgive ourselves. We will include the situation on the chart, journal our feelings, ask God for forgiveness, and work through the process of forgiving ourselves. Then, in the future, if we find ourselves remembering past sins and sinking into self-condemnation, we can refer back to this chart and remind ourselves of the freedom we experienced through forgiving ourselves.

Begin now to work through the chart. Remember, forgiveness is an ongoing process. It will not be completed in an hour, a day, a week, or even a month. Feel free to make copies of this appendix and use it as a lifelong tool to keep you on the road to emotional healing and forgiveness.

As Jesus Sees. . .You

So many of us stay stuck in self-condemnation because we have never seen true forgiveness modeled for us by our parents or friends or in other relationships in our lives. When we don't see compassion in action, it is difficult to grasp the depths of God's mercy and grace. Like a jeep churning its wheels in the mud, we spin faster and faster and faster, going nowhere in our relationships because we can't say simple words such as "I'm sorry" or "Will you forgive me?" We don't realize that if we choose (and it is a choice) to live a life of condemnation, blame, and attack, then we suffer many things, including these:

- Hindered prayers
- Severed relationships
- A squelched spiritual life
- A diminished witness
- Blindness to the truth
- Bondage to sin, loneliness, and despair
- A bitter, angry spirit

• Great risk for heart disease, heart attack, stroke, and depression

None of these paints a picture of the abundant life God desires for us. The apostle John promises, "If we confess our sins, he is faithful and just and will forgive us our sins and purify us from all unrighteousness" (1 John 1:9). Through confession, we experience forgiveness. Through forgiveness, we experience purification. Through purification, we experience righteousness in the One who came to save us. Isn't that worth saying, "Will you forgive me?"

We cannot change the past. We cannot restore lives back exactly the way they were. We can, however, pray for reconciliation and Christ-centered restoration. After Jesus prayed for His Father to forgive the very people who were killing Him on the cross, He made one final gesture of compassion and forgiveness to a humble, repentant criminal.

> *One of the criminals who hung there hurled insults at him: "Aren't you the Messiah? Save yourself and us!" But the other criminal rebuked him. "Don't you fear God," he said, "since you are under the same sentence? We are punished justly, for we are getting what our deeds deserve. But this man has done nothing wrong."*
>
> *Then he said, "Jesus, remember me when you come into your kingdom."*
>
> *Jesus answered him, "Truly I tell you, today you will be with me in paradise."*
>
> Luke 23:39–43

Sometimes we are like the first criminal, hurling insults at each other when we don't get our way, doubting God's goodness, His plan, and even His deity. Other times we are like the second criminal, living in our final moments, gasping for our final breath, and clinging to more of Jesus and less of this world. My guess is that most days we are a mixture of both men: feeling the pull of the nails in our hands, the sweat on our brows, and the disappointment from a wearisome life dragging us down into the abyss of our own defeat and despair, yet desperately longing to be with Jesus in paradise.

The first criminal saw himself as the world saw him—despicable, insignificant, unforgivable. The second criminal saw himself as Jesus saw him—worthy, valuable, forgivable—and it changed him for eternity. My friend, if you could see as Jesus sees, through His lens of forgiveness, how would it change you? Would you see yourself as the first criminal? Or as the second? Take some time to journal your thoughts below.

_____

_____

_____

_____

_____

_____

_____

_____

_____

_____

_____

_____

_____

_____

_____

Elizabeth Oates

As Jesus Sees. . .Your Relationships

If you could see as Jesus sees, through His lens of forgiveness, how would this affect your relationships? Would your friendships be deeper, healthier, more meaningful? Would your marriage be stronger? Would you have more open dialogue with your children and/or your parents? Feel free to journal your thoughts in the space provided.

_____

_____

_____

_____

_____

As Jesus Sees. . .Your Community

If you could see as Jesus sees, through His lens of forgiveness, how would this affect your community? Would you engage more in the world around you? Would you open yourself up to new experiences without the fear of getting hurt by others? Would you show more compassion and less judgment toward others? Take a moment to journal about past and present experiences.

_____

_____

_____

_____

_____

As Jesus Sees. . .Your Relationship with God

If you could see as Jesus sees, through His lens of forgiveness, how would that change your relationship with your heavenly Father? Would you find peace and comfort in knowing that God sent His only Son to die in order to make this forgiveness possible for you? Would you want to offer God gratitude and adoration? Feel free to do that now. End with a prayer of thanksgiving for all God has done for you on this journey as you have switched your lens from seeing yourself as the world sees you to seeing yourself as your Savior sees. Praise God for being ever-present and making the path to forgiveness possible through His Son, Jesus Christ.

_____

_____

_____

_____

_____

_____

_____

_____

_____

_____

_____

_____

_____

Personal Reflection Questions

1. How was, "I'm sorry" and forgiveness handled when you were a child?

    -   How has that shaped your current views on forgiveness?

    _____

    _____

    _____

    _____

    _____

    _____

2. Elizabeth writes, "When people insult us, we forgive them. When they question our credentials and identity, we forgive them. When they seek to destroy our spirits and souls, we forgive them. When they take our possessions, we forgive them. When they try to isolate us, we forgive them. When they hate us, we forgive them. When they condemn us, we forgive them." How difficult is this for you? Explain.

    _____

    _____

    _____

    _____

    _____

    _____

3. Elizabeth writes, "Forgiveness is a choice. Much like love. And it does not always come naturally or easily." Does forgiveness come easily or naturally for you? Explain why or why not.

_____

_____

_____

_____

_____

_____

4. In this chapter Elizabeth poses the question, "Do you feel God calling you to forgive someone, yet you can't bring yourself to take that step?" If you do feel that God is calling you to forgive someone, write that person's name (or initials or code name) in the space provided. After working through the chapter, are you better able to forgive that person? If not, do you know what is holding you back? Journal your thoughts in the space provided.

_____

_____

_____

_____

_____

_____

5. Are you currently wrestling with a situation where you find it difficult to forgive yourself? If so, explain in the space below. Jesus has already died on the cross so that all your sins (including the one with which you are wrestling) could be forgiven. What else would need to happen before you could forgive yourself?

_____

_____

_____

_____

_____

_____

6. With whom do you identify more, the criminal who asked to be with Jesus in paradise or the other criminal?

_____

_____

_____

_____

_____

_____

_____

_____

_____

Group Reflection Questions

1. How was saying "I'm sorry" and forgiveness handled when you were a child?

    • How has that shaped your current views on forgiveness?

2. Looking at Elizabeth's definition of forgiveness, is there anything you'd add to it? Explain.

3. Elizabeth writes, "When people insult us, we forgive them. When they question our credentials and identity, we forgive them. When they seek to destroy our spirits and souls, we forgive them. When they take our possessions, we forgive them. When they try to isolate us, we forgive them. When they hate us, we forgive them. When they condemn us, we forgive them." How difficult is this for you? Explain.

4. Elizabeth writes, "Forgiveness is a choice. Much like love. And it does not always come naturally or easily." Does forgiveness come easily or naturally for you? Explain why or why not.

5. Elizabeth listed several reasons why we might not be able to forgive someone. Did any of these resonate with you? If so, which ones?

6. You also read a list of reasons why we don't forgive ourselves. Which of these reasons apply to you?

7. Did you work through the "If We Could Forgive and Not Forget" chart? What where your thoughts on that?

8. With whom do you identify more, the criminal who asked to be with Jesus in paradise or the other criminal?

Appendix A
As Jesus Sees. . .Me

Take your time in filling out the chart on the next page. The first row has been filled in as an example, but the rest have been left blank for you to fill out. Feel free to write directly on the page or make copies of the page and add on as needed. Fill in as many "flaws" (which we know are not truly flaws but are only perceived as such because we are seeing them through the world's eyes and not through Jesus' eyes) as you want. Continue adding to this chart as you work through the book. There is no time limit on the chart. Take an hour, a day, a week, a month, or continue to add to it every time you hear the whisper of the enemy telling you that some personal feature is not quite good enough. When we write down our flawed thinking, we are able to see the lies we tell ourselves and see as Jesus sees.

My "Flaw"	My New Lens
Right now I see my _____ as _____.	If I could see my _____ as Jesus sees my_____, then I would see it as _____.
Right now I see my hair as thin and frail and boring.	If I could see my hair as Jesus sees my hair, then I would see it as brown, beautiful, not too thick, not too thin, and easy to manage. It is great because I can wear it straight or curly. It is perfect for my personality type because it doesn't take too long to dry, and I am a very impatient person. (God knew I couldn't handle having thick hair that would take a long time to dry.)

My Commitment	My Change
Now that I see my _____ as Jesus sees my _____, I will _____.	How am I now changed?
Now that I see my hair as Jesus sees my hair, I will be thankful for it. He gave me the perfect hair for my face shape, my body type, and my personality type. Many women are struggling with medical hair loss or cancer, so I am grateful that I even have hair. Gone are the days of me complaining about not having thick hair!	I am changed because I now realize my hair is part of God's design for me. God designed it this particular way for a reason, and I have been foolishly wasting time wishing it were a different way. Lord, please forgive me for my nearsightedness. Forgive me for wanting anything less than Your best. Help me find beauty in every part of myself because every part of myself is Your creation.

Appendix B
The Fallacy of Inadequacy

On the next page is a chart to help us work through our history of unmet expectations to see how they lead us to look continually through our lens of inadequacy. The first row has been filled in as an example, but the rest have been left blank for you to fill out. Feel free to write directly on the page or make copies of the page and add on as needed.

As you work through your memories of unmet expectations, you will see a pattern of your emotional and spiritual reactions. The goal is for you to better understand how you respond to unmet expectations so you can respond in a healthy way and see yourself through Jesus' lens of acceptance.

Expectation	Outcome	Feeling (Confident, inadequate, peaceful, shaken, etc.)
I was up for a promotion and fully expected to get it.	I did not get the promotion; instead, someone else in my department received it.	I felt disappointed, frustrated, and completely inadequate. I wondered why I put in the long hours I do when clearly I am not appreciated. I considered looking for employment elsewhere.

How it affected my relationship with God (Did you trust Him, turn from Him, etc.?)	Pattern of inadequacy and commitment to change
I was mad at God because I felt like He owed this to me. Then I realized He doesn't owe me anything, so I was just mad. But it is still difficult for me to trust that He is doing what is best for me. I don't see how staying stuck in my current position is best for me.	I realize that I often set an expectation. When that expectation is not met, I feel inadequate and rejected. Then I spiral downward and want to run away. Instead of running away, I am committing to run toward God so that I can begin to see myself through His lens of acceptance.

Appendix C
God's Provisions

Below is a chart to help us remember all the ways in which God has provided for us in the past. The purpose of filling out the chart is three-fold:

1. To help you remember God's faithfulness.
2. To give you something concrete to look back on when you doubt God's goodness and faithfulness in your life.
3. To show you all the blessings you already have so that when discontentment creeps into your heart, you can squelch it with the abundance of blessings God has already given you.

The first row has been filled in as an example, but the rest have been left blank for you to fill out. Feel free to write directly on the page or make copies of this page and add on as needed.

Age (childhood, adulthood, present)	Situation	How God Provided
Adulthood	When we were trying to pay off our mountain of student loans, we received a random $800 check from a previous employer.	It was just a drop in the bucket compared to the thousands upon thousands of dollars we owed in student loans, but I felt like God was saying, "I'm right here with you. I see how hard you're trying, and I'll be with you every step of the way."

Appendix D
If We Could Forgive and Not Forget

Situation	Sin committed against me (place a check)	Sin committed by me (place a check)
Example: I gossiped about my friend, which led to some hurt feelings, including a rift within a group of friends.		✓

Deeper issues that motivated the behaviors leading to the sin	Journal my thoughts and feelings
I am insecure about myself and especially within this group of friends. I realize I need to find my confidence in Christ and also find security in my social circle.	Jesus, I realize in hindsight that what I did was wrong. The Bible tells us not to gossip. This is such junior high behavior, and yet I went there. What was I thinking? I apologized to everyone involved. Some have chosen to forgive me and some have not. Even though I was not the only one at fault, I seem to be the only one being persecuted. I can't think about the injustice of that because the truth is I was in the wrong. So I pray that You will help me continue to love these women. Help me to continue extending my hand in love and forgiveness. Help me to continue to show them that I can be trustworthy. Help me avoid seeing myself in the same light in which they see me. Help me resist defining myself by this one mistake. Help me to cling to Your truth, which is that in Christ I am a new creation. Amen.

Notes

Chapter 1. My Lens of Self Loathing, His Lens of Love

1. Glennon Doyle Melton, "When Craig and I Separated," July 18, 2014, accessed August 3, 2015. http://momastery.com/ blog/2014/07/18/when-craig-and-i-separated/.

Chapter 2. My Lens of Ugliness, His Lens of Beauty

1. http://www.raderprograms.com/causes-statistics/media-eating-disorders.html. Accessed August 10, 2014.
2. "The Facts," Confidence Coalition, Kappa Delta Sorority, accessed August 24, 2014, http://confidencecoalition.org/statistics-women.
3. "Beauty at Any Cost," YWCA, accessed August 21, 2014. http://www. ywca.org/atf/cf/ percent7B711d5519-9e3c-4362-b753-ad138b5d352c percent7D/BEAUTY-AT-ANY-COST.pdf .
4. "The American Society for Aesthetic Plastic Surgery Reports Americans Spent More Than 12 Billion in 2014; Procedures for Men Up 43% Over Five Year Period," American Society for Aesthetic Plastic Surgery, accessed May 25, 2015. http://www.surgery.org/media/ news-releases/the-american-society-for-aesthetic-plastic-surgery-reports-americans-spent-largest-amount-on-cosmetic-surgery.
5. Ibid.
6. Jillian Lauren, "This Is How I Begin," *Huffington Post,* November 17, 2013, accessed August 3, 2015. http://www.huffingtonpost.com/jillian-lauren/this-is-how-i-begin_b_3936478.html.

Chapter 3. My Lens of Shame, His Lens of Redemption

1. Brené Brown, quoted by Jessie Sholl, "Shutting Shame Down," *Experience L!fe*, October 2013, https://experiencelife.com/article/shutting-shame-down/.
2. Ibid.
3. Sholl, "Shutting Shame Down."
4. "Shame," Dictionary.com, http://dictionary.reference.com/browse/ shame?s=t.
5. Tyler Charles, "The Secret Sexual Revolution," *Relevant*, February 20, 2012, http://www.relevantmagazine.com/life/relationship/features/28337-the-secret-sexual-revolution.
6. "Induced Abortion in the United States," Guttmacher Institute, July 2014, accessed August 23, 2014, http://www.guttmacher.org/pubs/ fb_induced_abortion.html.